SHAVE
10 STROKES
IN **12** DAYS

SHAVE **10** STROKES IN **12** DAYS

A Woman Golfer's Guide to a More Successful Game

SANDY LABAUVE
LPGA, PGA Teaching Professional

AND GEORGE KEHOE
Editor, *Golf for Women* Magazine

Photographs by Tony Armstrong, Sea Island Photography

A PERIGEE BOOK

Perigee Books
are published by
The Berkley Publishing Group
200 Madison Avenue
New York, NY 10016

Library of Congress Cataloging-in-Publication Data
LaBauve, Sandy.
    Shave 10 strokes in 12 days : a woman golfer's guide to a more
successful game / Sandy LaBauve and George Kehoe.
        p.   cm.
    ISBN 0-399-51860-6
    1. Golf for women.   I. Kehoe, George.   II. Title.   III. Title:
Shave ten strokes in twelve days.
GV966.L32 1994   93-45041   CIP
796.352—dc20

Cover design by Richard Rossiter
Cover photograph © by Tony Armstrong/Sea Island Photography

Printed in the United States of America
1 2 3 4 5 6 7 8 9 10

This book is printed on acid-free paper.

⊗

To Michael, my husband, who's a wonderful teaching professional, and to my daughters, Lindy and Kristi, who I hope will someday play golf.

And to . . .
My father, who's a pro
My brother, who's a pro
My sister, who used to be a pro
Her husband, who's a pro
Mike's brother-in-law, who's a pro
My grandfather, who should have been a pro
My aunt, who used to be a pro
My uncle, who plays like a pro
And my mom, who definitely could have been a pro

I promise to keep the tradition alive by making golf more fun to learn.

Special thanks to Sea Island Golf Club, Sea Island, Georgia.

Contents

On Your Mark, Get Set, Go!

If you're like most women I teach, you fit golf into a busy schedule that juggles career and family life. You play golf to interact with friends, get some exercise, and perhaps complement your business. And, indeed, your performance on the course is very important. Although becoming the world's greatest golfer may not be your goal, you certainly want to play respectably and feel comfortable teeing it up with anyone.

That's what this 12-day program is all about. By actively participating, you'll cover all the elements needed to build a reliable golf swing and a competent golf game. As you achieve more consistency in your swing, more distance in your long game, and more feel in your short game, you'll see your scores improve significantly. By interspersing practice at the course with drills you can do at home, the program's schedule is thorough yet reasonable in terms of time.

During the next 12 days, we'll address your game from four specific angles:

• *Gaining Distance:* Hitting the ball farther translates into fewer shots to reach the green. You'll hit less club into the green more often and, consequently, hit your ball closer to the hole. Of course, distance isn't worth much without accuracy. Stick with the program and you'll hit the ball more consistently on the sweet spot of the clubface and make your shotmaking more predictable.

• *Putting Your Ball Up and In:* Putting just isn't that difficult. It takes no strength and requires very little stroke. But wow! It sure does account for a bagful of strokes during a round. We're going to turn putting into a steady source of strength in your game.

• *Short-Game Stroke Savers:* When we're through, you'll know the difference between a chip, a pitch, and a lob and know which club to use for what shot. You'll also learn to play from uneven lies and blast from the sand with confidence.

• *Playing Smart Golf:* Learn how to better manage your game on the course as you learn to better prepare for each shot. We'll also find ways to make improving more fun. What's more, my 40-minute practice program will prove invaluable in helping you take strokes off your score and keep them off.

At the end of each chapter, you'll find a reference sheet that summarizes the day's program and offers swing keys to help you remember what to do. This review is a great tool. You may want to copy these pages and carry them in your golf bag to help keep you on the right track.

Each day's lesson also includes drills and exercises to do at the practice range and some homework to do in front of a mirror. The homework reinforces what you're trying to do on the course and helps check your progress. Once you know what to look for, you can almost coach yourself. My motto is: "Mirror mirror on the wall, make me a golfer after all." Adopt it! It works.

As the days unfold, personalize your program and set goals based on your strengths and weaknesses. All I ask is that you make a plan. If you don't have one, follow mine. If you don't know where you're going, you'll probably wind up somewhere else.

THE EQUIPMENT FACTOR

Before you get started, get ready by having an equipment checkup. If your clubs aren't right for you, it's going to be a lot tougher to drop those 10 shots. Put the odds in your favor and check out these six major specifications with a trained clubfitter:

• *Grip size:* If the grips on your clubs are too big, you may not be able to use enough hand action in your swing. If the grips are too small, you may overuse your hands. If your grips are worn, holding onto the club throughout your swing may prove difficult and increase tension.

• *Shaft length:* If too long, you'll likely swing your club too much around your body and lose ball flight control. If too short, you'll probably swing your club too much up and down and lose distance. In either case, your setup will be out of kilter.

• *Shaft flex:* If too stiff, you'll tend to hit the ball lower than normal and to the right. If too flexible, you'll tend to hit the ball higher than normal and either left or right.

• *Lie angle:* If too upright, you'll tend to hit the ball to the left of your target. If too flat, you'll tend to hit the ball to the right of your target.

• *Club design:* You'll probably do best with irons that are cavity-backed and perimeter-weighted. (Older clubs don't have these features.) The benefits are straightforward. You can mis-hit your shots more off-center and still get reasonably good distance and direction.

• *Set makeup:* Definitely include a sand wedge through five-iron. Consider a four- or three-iron if you're a good long-iron player, or substitute a seven-wood for the four-iron and a six-wood for the three-iron if you prefer woods. Also, consider adding a third wedge to expand your short-game repertoire. For off the tee, select a driving club that allows you to get adequate distance and still keep your ball in play. A three-wood loft is often best.

Your body will naturally try to make compensations in your swing to counteract improperly fit equipment. You may drop shots off your score just by making adjustments to your clubs. Now, wouldn't that be easy?

So let's get with the program. On your mark: make your plan. Get set: check your clubs. Go . . .

DAY 1

The Grip and the Setup

Most of the power in your swing comes from a sound body pivot, a good wrist cock, and an effective sequence of motion. To pivot correctly, you need an athletic setup when addressing the ball. To cock your wrists in the backswing without having your hands come off the club, you need a grip that not only allows but also encourages the hands to work together—a compatible grip. To achieve an effective sequence of motion, you must blend the movements of your hands, arms, and body to create a fluid swing. We'll get into how to do that later. Let's start with your grip.

THE COMPATIBLE GRIP

Initiating your grip with your right hand makes it easier to see that your clubface is lined up properly. Take the club in your right hand, holding it near the shaft and straight out in front of you, making sure the leading edge is perpendicular to the ground. The toe of the club should point up. When you lower the club to the ground, the leading edge should be perpendicular to your intended target line. You now have a square clubface.

Keeping the club in front of you, pre-mold your left hand by placing the thumb and forefinger close together until a "V" is formed. As the rest of your fingers naturally begin to curve around, slip your hand onto the club so the heel of your hand rests on top of the club handle, then close your fingers so the club is secure. Hold the club at an angle between the joints in your forefinger and the heel of your hand, and feel most of the pressure in your last three fingers. The "V" points at your right shoulder. You should be able to see two knuckles clearly.

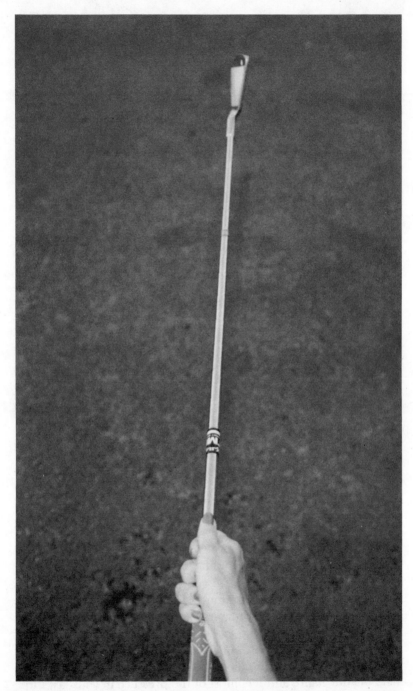

Hold the club straight out with your right hand so the leading edge is perpendicular to the ground and the toe is straight up.

When lowered to the ground, the clubface should be perpendicular to your intended target line.

Club rests at an angle between finger joints and heel pad.

The "V" points at your right shoulder. You should be able to see two knuckles clearly.

Next, slide your right hand down and connect with your left. To complete your grip at this point, you've got three choices to consider:

- the overlap grip, good for normal to large hands, is the most popular with professionals and the one I use;
- the 10-finger grip, with all fingers on the club, is ideal for tiny or weak hands;
- the interlock grip is ideal for hands with shorter fingers.

Try all three and select one. Usually one of them will feel better almost instantly.

The club rests in the fingers of the right hand at an angle, with pressure predominantly in the middle two fingers. Again, the "V" formed with your thumb and forefinger points at your right shoulder. Note how the two "Vs" are parallel. That's a good sign that your hands will work together, and that's the essence of a compatible grip.

The overlap grip.

The 10-finger grip.

The interlock grip.

The two "Vs" are parallel
and pointing toward your
right shoulder in the correct
grip.

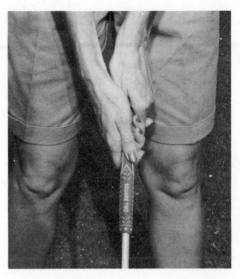

You should be aware that women often have a hard time getting
the left hand far enough to the right on the club because of our
chests. Although it may feel awkward, placing your left hand over is
a stronger position. Your right hand won't have to overcontrol the
clubface, and your wrists will be able to cock more freely.

A note about grip pressure: Hold the club securely enough that it
won't slip in your fingers but relaxed enough so your wrists are free
to cock. At address, your arms should hang from your body and not
be locked up. Too much tension inhibits wrist action, and that
translates into loss of power. We're into gaining distance here, not
losing it!

Find the grip pressure best for you by working through this little
formula: Hold onto a club as tightly as you can and call that grip
pressure Level 5. Loosen your hold a little and call that Level 4.
Loosen your hold a bit more for Level 3, and so on until you work
your way down to Level 1, a very light grip. You should play most of
your golf shots with a Level 3 grip pressure.

THE ATHLETIC SETUP

An athletic setup blends balance, comfort, and readiness—not
tenseness—as you address the ball. Stand tall with your feet
shoulder-distance apart for irons, perhaps slightly wider for woods.

Bend from the hips, keeping your head, neck, and spine in a relatively straight line. You'll probably have a slight "cup" in your back, and that's all right. Flex your knees and think "Head up, rear out."

When properly aligned, your shoulders, hips, and feet are parallel to each other and parallel left of your target line. That means they aren't aimed at your target but left of it. If your body is aimed at your target, your arms have no choice but to swing to the right because your body is in the way.

To quickly check your posture, hold a club against your back and bend from the hips without letting your body leave the club. The middle of your shoulders, your knees, and the balls of your feet should be in a relatively straight line.

A good, athletic setup may feel funny to some because we've been taught all our lives to stick our rears under and keep our heads down. Doing so makes you bend from the top of your back, which stifles your ability to pivot. Remember, as awkward as it feels: rear out, chin up.

You should feel your weight on the balls of your feet and feel balanced like you are ready and free to move. For most shots, your weight is evenly distributed between both feet. However, you may want to favor your right side for longer clubs and your left side for less-than-full shots.

Arms hang out and down from your body, resting slightly on top of your chest. Elbows are fairly close together and arms extended so they create a triangle with your shoulders. Your right side is lower because your right hand is lower on the club.

The ball should be positioned toward the left heel for tee shots. Play it two to three inches inside the left heel for long irons or fairway woods and slightly ahead of the center of your stance for short irons. Just remember, the longer the club, the more forward in your stance you play the ball.

HOMEWORK

• Grip the club in front of a mirror, checking to make sure you create parallel "Vs" and that your grip matches mine in the photos. After you see that it is correct, close your eyes and try to feel where you've placed your hands on the club. Connect what you see with what you feel. Open your eyes and repeat for five minutes.

Your body should not leave the club.

A straight line should run from the middle of your shoulders, through your knees, to the balls of your feet.

Note how the right side of my body is lower than the left. This makes sense because my right hand is lower on the club.

• Practice your grip while watching a 30-minute TV show. During the commercials, look down at your club and carefully mold your hands around the handle. When the show comes on, continue to grip the club while watching the program. Don't look at your hands; simply feel your hands molding correctly. When the commercials return, recheck your hand positions until the show comes back on. Watch the rest of the show without glancing down as the repetitions help groove your grip. Your hands may get a little tired, but I guarantee you'll feel more comfortable with where your hands belong on your club in just 30 minutes.

• Practice your posture in front of a mirror. Face the mirror, checking to make sure that your right side is set slightly lower than your left. Try to match the posture in my photos. Now turn to the side and check to make sure you appear balanced, with the middle of your shoulders, knees, and balls of your feet in the same line. Close your eyes and feel the correct posture. Open your eyes and look again. Ingrain the picture in your mind and connect what you see with what you feel. Do it the right way, then do it the wrong way. It helps to see and feel the difference. Spend at least five minutes in front of the mirror. Refer to my photos or tape copies to your mirror to help keep you on track.

DRILLS FOR THE PRACTICE TEE

• Warm up: Always warm up first by stretching and hitting 5–10 short irons at a target.

• Hit 20 balls with an eight-iron. Re-grip your club before you hit each shot. Start every time with the club in your right hand out in front of you. Then grip with the left, and slide your right hand down.

• Hit 10 balls with a five-iron, checking your posture before each shot. Hold a club either behind your back or vertically to your side, making sure the middle of your shoulders, your knees, and the balls of your feet are relatively in the same line. Think "Spread my feet in one, bend from my hips in two, and flex my knees in three."

• Hit five balls each with an eight-iron, a five-iron, and your driving club off a tee. Set up a practice station with two perpendicular

The eight-iron station.

The five-iron station.

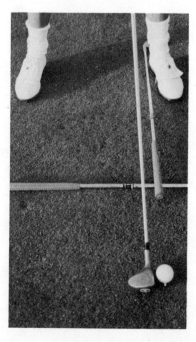

The tee shot station.

clubs so you can make sure your ball position is good and your feet are parallel to your target line. Place one club parallel left of your target line, the other even with your ball. (You may choose to hit all balls off a tee for this drill so you don't have to continuously reset your station.) Practicing this way also improves your alignment.

• Finish by hitting five balls with a six-iron and try not to think about anything. Trust your grip and your setup, and leave the practice tee with a smile. This is just the beginning.

REFERENCE SHEET: DAY 1

THE GRIP AND THE SETUP

COMPATIBLE GRIP

- Square the clubface with your right hand by holding the club out in front of you.
- Pre-mold your left hand and slide it on the club with the heel of your hand on top of the club handle.
- Left "V" points at your right shoulder.
- Slide right hand down and connect with left.
- Club rests more in your fingers than in your palms.
- Right "V" is parallel to left "V" and points at your right shoulder.
- Grip pressure is adequate to hold onto the club but arms are not locked.
- Use a Level 3 grip pressure.
- Hands work together as a unit.

ATHLETIC SETUP

- Feet shoulder-distance apart for irons, slightly wider for woods.
- Feet, shoulders, and hips are parallel to each other and parallel left of your intended target.
- Bend from your hips, keeping head, neck, and back in a relatively straight line.
- Arms form a triangle with the shoulders.
- Right side is set slightly lower than left.
- Weight is evenly distributed for most clubs.
- The longer the club, the farther forward you play the ball in your stance.

SWING KEYS

"Parallel Vs in your grip."

"Rear out, chin up."

"Balanced and athletic."

"Ready to move."

"Feel powerful."

DAY 2

Pivot to Create Power

To add distance to your golf shots, you must use the small, speed-producing muscles in your hands and arms together with the larger muscles in your upper body and legs. Your hands, arms, and body must work in sync. If your hands and arms go one way while your body goes another, your ball could fly anywhere. A good body pivot coordinates the power in your swing. Let's get a picture of the entire swing and see how the pivot fits in.

Think of swinging your club in a circular fashion up and around your body. Whatever you do on the right side, you want to do on the left. Your hands and arms swing the club up and down as your body turns back and through. Simply blend the proper amount of up-and-down motion with the around motion of your body, add a sense of rhythm so the swing flows, and you've got it. The pivot is what makes it all go.

Always keep in mind that you are making a swing, and the ball is struck within the swing. You are not just trying to hit a ball. If you think *hit* instead of *swing*, you may get chop and flop instead!

INTO THE WINDUP

The pivot begins with your body windup, the artful movement of your upper torso twisting against the lower body in the backswing. You're trying to turn your upper body twice as much as your lower body to create "torque." Whether you call it turning, coiling, or something else, the pivot is what enables you to shift your weight and move your power behind the ball. It gets you set up to move into the shot with power, and that turns into distance.

If you don't wind up with the big muscles of your torso and legs, you'll strike the ball with only the power of your hands and arms.

In the circular swing, the hands and arms swing up and down as the body turns back and through.

You may hit it straight every time, but you won't hit it very far, and you'll probably wear yourself out in the process. Have you ever finished a round totally exhausted, feeling like you worked so hard and didn't get much for your effort? Chances are, you used too much arm swing and not enough body.

The arm-swing tendency is common among women golfers because we often don't begin with an athletic setup. Thus, our body is in the way from the start, and we end up swinging with our arms. We think we're turning because our arms either swing too far around our bodies or they lift straight up. Either way, our weight doesn't shift properly.

Imagine, if you will, that you're going to give a sidearm "spanking" and you're really mad! If you use just your hands and arms, you'll merely deliver a glancing blow. Using your hands, arms, *and* body supplies the force.

THE TURN BACK

From a good setup, begin turning your left shoulder and torso as your hands and arms start to swing the club away from the ball. This is commonly known as the one-piece takeaway. Arms, hands, left shoulder, and club all go back together. Your head will move a little bit, and that's okay. The one-piece takeaway gets you swinging in proper sync.

Your hips and lower body are your base and don't turn until they're pulled around by the turning of your shoulders and torso.

At the top of the swing, your left shoulder should be turned over your right thigh, and your back should be facing your intended target. If your left heel comes up a little, that's fine. Your weight— 70 percent now on your right side—has transferred from the balls of your feet to the inside heel of your right foot and the toe of your left foot. If, instead, your weight moves to both heels, your shoulders are probably turning too level. If your weight moves to the outsides of both feet, you're more than likely swaying. If your weight favors your left heel and right toe, you are probably reverse pivoting. And if your weight moves to both toes, you may be dipping.

Now, don't get all caught up with your feet, but do use them as a checkpoint. Every so often, check how your weight is distributed throughout your swing and let your feet clue you in as to whether or not you are pivoting correctly.

"Spanking" with hands, arms, and body gives you full force.

Take the club away in one piece. Begin turning your left shoulder and torso as your hands and arms swing the club back.

At the top of the backswing, strive to turn your left shoulder over your right thigh. Your torso has turned twice as much as your hips, and your back faces the target. Your spine angle is maintained.

Watch out for these common errors:

• Don't start your swing with a hip turn. If you do, chances are you'll swing the club too much behind you, then have to lift it at the top of your backswing. Often, the result is a reverse pivot.

• Don't pick the club up too fast and forget to turn your shoulders in the takeaway. This produces either a reverse pivot or a shoulder dip. In both cases, you wind up over the wrong leg and never get your power behind the ball, so you can't possibly get the distance you would with a proper weight shift. Now, I ask you, who can afford to sacrifice 20 to 30 yards off the tee?

• Don't exaggerate your weight shift by moving your hips from side to side either. This creates the lateral motion known as the "dreaded sway." Again, you get a false feeling of turning. You more or less create a "rock-and-block" weight shift—which sends the ball to the right of your target—instead of a pivot that helps you hit the

When hips turn first, the club often swings behind you. Your shoulders never catch up or turn properly.

In the reverse pivot, your torso winds up over the left leg instead of the right, which results in a major loss of distance.

ball straight and far. Moving off the ball totally also makes it hard to return to the ball in a position similar to that at address. You can only imagine what that does to your consistency.

When you bend properly at the hips, your shoulders turn on a 90-degree angle from your spine. You want to maintain your spine angle at the top of your backswing. Your left shoulder turns under your chin. If you get makeup on your shirt during your swing, chances are your shoulders are turning too level to the ground, and you are losing your spine angle.

When you move laterally going back, you move off the ball too much. There is no windup, so it's impossible to unwind.

If you sway coming through, you'll have a difficult time hitting the ball straight. There isn't enough "around" motion with your body, and your upper body gets too far out in front of your lower body. This is the "rock-and-block" syndrome.

Your shoulders turn perpendicular to your spine. If you place a club behind your shoulders and turn, it should point just beyond the ball at the top of your backswing. (Notice how the head of the club is not pointing at or inside the ball, a common mistake.) Maintain your spine angle at the top of your swing.

If you're in good shape at the top of the backswing, you should feel torque between your upper and lower body. At that point in my swing, I feel a pull in the left side of my back and resistance in my right knee. When I don't feel that tension, I know my pivot is off, and I keep winding up my upper torso against my hips until I can feel it again to get back on track.

If you find it difficult to make a full turn on the backswing, consider doing flexibility exercises to help stretch your back muscles so you can turn more freely. Remember, more pivot means more power and distance. Here are two of my favorite exercises:

Trunk rotation: Keeping your hips and legs stationary, rotate your upper body while holding a club waist high as far to one side as you can, keeping shoulders level and abdominal muscles contracted. Hold to the count of five. Repeat on the other side. Do this exercise 10 times daily.

Shoulder rotation stretch: Reach down your back grasping a club in your left hand and reach up to the club with your right hand. Walk hands as close together as you can comfortably. Hold 10–15 seconds, then walk hands a little closer and hold to the count of five. Reverse your hands and repeat. Do this exercise five times daily.

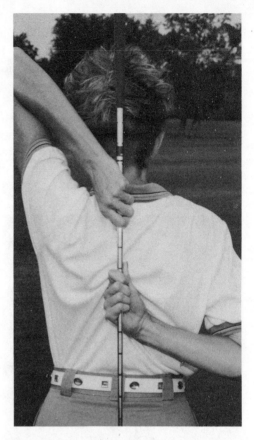

In the meantime, you can compensate a little by either slightly turning your right foot out at address, which allows your hips to turn a little more on the backswing; moving your head a couple more inches; or lifting your left heel up higher. Any of these adjustments increases your ability to move, but also increases your chances of making mistakes because they add motion to your swing.

THE TURN THROUGH

If you wind up properly in the backswing, the downswing—the unwinding—will be a piece of cake. It's action and reaction. You simply release the tension (torque) by turning your lower body to the left as your arms and hands pull the club down toward the ball. Note how I said "pull" and not "throw" the club toward the ball. That means the club handle swings down before the clubhead.

Continue to turn through until your shoulders face left of your target and hips face the target. Arms and hands finish up above your left shoulder. Your right shoulder is lower than your left because it has passed under your chin. About 90 percent of your weight is on the left heel and 10 percent is on the right toe. Your right heel has been pulled off the ground. You feel balanced like you're on the top of a trophy. What an awesome feeling!

If you have trouble turning all the way through, start with your left foot turned out about 15 degrees at address. This helps free up your hip socket so you can turn through your shot more easily. If your problem is turning through too much, point your left toe straight ahead at address to restrict your hip movement in the turn through.

Remember, pivot means power. Whenever you need distance, you need pivot. Of course, you won't need as much for a chip shot as for, say, a full three-iron. On shorter shots, your focus is on making the ball go to a nearby target rather than on hitting it far. Use more body when you need distance and less when you want less.

Does every position have to be perfectly correct? Absolutely not! Just remember the concept: turn back, turn through, and feel weight shift. Learning to pivot will improve your woods and long irons. You'll quit slicing the ball so much and gain 20–30 yards in distance. Just think "Less shots per hole, more irons into greens, balls closer to the hole, two shots less per round." You're on your way!

HOMEWORK

• Practice turning your shoulders perpendicular to your spine in front of a mirror. Hold a club horizontally behind your shoulders and twist. Do this drill face on and from the side, looking at your pivot from both angles. See what a correct pivot looks like, then close your eyes and feel what a correct pivot feels like. Think about where you feel tension when you create torque between your upper and lower body so you can look for those checkpoints at the course. Spend about 10 minutes pivoting correctly.

In the balanced finish, 90 percent of your weight is on the left heel. Right heel is up. Shoulders face left of your target. Hips face target. Right shoulder is lower than the left.

Note how the hands and arms are above the left shoulder.

• If swaying has been a problem, practice in front of your mirror by placing a dot of lipstick on the mirror marking your right hip. Turn back without allowing your hips to move past the lipstick.

DRILLS FOR THE PRACTICE TEE

• Warm up by putting a club behind your shoulders, getting into your athletic setup, and twisting back and through. When you turn back, the club should stay perpendicular to your spine and the clubhead should point just beyond the ball as in my photo. Do this 25 times, then hit a few warm-up balls with a short iron.

• Practice your one-piece takeaway without hitting a ball. Simply swing the club back from the ball about three feet, feeling your left shoulder, hands, arms, and club going back together. Repeat about 10 times.

• Hit 45 balls with a five-iron, concentrating on your pivot before each shot. Between every five balls, make a practice swing and pause at the top: You want 70 percent of your weight on your right heel and 30 percent on your left toe, your left shoulder turned over your right thigh, and your back facing the target. Now swing through and feel your weight shift. Hold your finish with 90 percent of your weight on your left side and feel balanced.

• Hit five balls without thinking about anything. Trust your compatible grip, your athletic setup, and your pivot. Just relax and take a couple of deep breaths before each shot.

PIVOT TO CREATE POWER

- Start with an athletic setup.
- Shoulders turn perpendicular to your spine.
- Wind up your left shoulder over your right thigh on the backswing.
- Your hips are your base and shouldn't move laterally on the backswing.
- Your hips turn half as much as your shoulders.
- Weight at the top of your swing is 70 percent on the right side.
- Unwinding starts by turning the left hip to the left and pulling the hands and arms toward the ball.
- Finish with hands and arms above your left shoulder.
- Your right shoulder is lower than your left.
- Shoulders face left of your target; hips face your target.
- Your weight is 90 percent on your left side.

SWING KEYS

"Turn back—turn through."

"Back to your target—front to your target."

"Wind up over your right—unwind over your left."

"Power back—power through."

"Action—reaction."

DAY 3

Arm Extension, Wrist Cock, and Clubface Rotation

In the circular swing, remember that your body has the job of pivoting, which helps your club to work around, while your hands and arms have the job of swinging the club up and down. Success depends on the proper blend of around motion and up-and-down motion. We must find how to do that! Today, let's concentrate on your arm swing, wrist cock, and how to rotate the club properly.

ARM EXTENSION

The key to good arm movement in the swing is extension. By extending your arms, you create width in your circular swing. With your arms extended, your wrists cock in the backswing and recock in the through swing while the clubface rotates in between. From the takeaway, your body turns so your arms can swing back on an arc. Of course, your arms begin in an extended position when you address the ball. They hang out and down from your body, forming a triangle with your shoulders, with your elbows fairly close together. The object is to swing back while keeping the triangle intact. This allows your arms to stay in front of you.

Now certainly your right arm eventually folds on the backswing and your left arm folds on the through swing. But just past impact, after you have struck the ball, your triangle is fully intact again. Your body must turn as you swing the club back and through or you will lift the club straight up and, consequently, come into the ball too steeply. This up-and-down swing shape produces pulled shots with the short irons, pop-ups with the driver, and a variety of slices, tops, fat shots, and toe shots with most any club. Sound familiar? You must swing the club up *and* around, so pivot as you extend your arms. Think turn and extend, turn and extend. Backswing, through swing.

Remember, arm extension with body pivot provides width to your swing. If your arms fold up, you make your swing arc very small, and the smaller the arc, the shorter the distance the ball will go. The wider the arc, the farther the ball will fly.

But don't get carried away with this; your arms needn't be stiff to extend. In fact, that's the last thing we want because stiff arms mean tense arms, and tense arms can't swing very fast. So don't get trapped into thinking left arm straight or "stiff." If it bends a little it

Turning your shoulder as your arms swing back keeps the club working up and around. Your right arm ultimately folds on the backswing.

Just past impact, your triangle—with extended arms—is once again intact.

After striking the ball, turn your body through and keep your arms extended. This keeps your swing circle wide and gives you distance. Your left arm ultimately folds on the through swing. Both arms fold at the finish.

won't matter; just extend as much as you can to keep your swing circle wide.

If, however, you can't extend your arms because the club feels too heavy, do some strength-building exercises for your upper body and wrists. Try these two:

Use 3- to 10-pound weights, depending on your current strength. Raise one weight at a time to shoulder height, twisting it as you come up. Do 15 repetitions on each side and do three sets. Increase your weight as this exercise becomes easier.

Use 3- to 5-pound weights, depending on your strength. Position your forearms parallel to the ground. Curl the weights—using both at the same time—up and down. Do 15 to 20 repetitions and do three sets. Again, increase weight as your strength increases.

WRIST COCK

The muscles in your hands and wrists may be small, but they can sure move fast. Wrist cock is leverage that gives you distance. Just try throwing a ball with no wrists, and then throwing with wrists. Your second attempt will go much farther with less effort. Now that's energy efficient!

But where in the swing should your wrists cock? There's no law, but I recommend you start cocking about three feet into the backswing and complete your wrist cock by the time the backswing is three-quarters done. If you cock your wrists too quickly, you'll likely pick the club up too fast and produce that up-and-down steep swing that causes slices and loss of distance. If you cock too late, you'll probably uncock too early on the downswing—known as "casting"—which also leads to steep swings and loss of distance.

The plan is to cock your wrists as you turn and extend your arms in the backswing. Then, as you initiate the forward swing, keep your

Complete your wrist cock by the time you are three-quarters into the backswing. Note how my shoulders are turning and my arms are extended.

Pull the club handle down from the top of the backswing toward the ball.

If you cock your wrists too late in the backswing, you'll probably "cast" from the top, which means your wrists will uncock too early in the downswing, resulting in a loss of power.

wrists cocked so you feel as though you're pulling the club instead of throwing it. Remember, "pull" means swinging the club handle down toward the ball first; "throw" means flinging the clubhead down first.

CLUBFACE ROTATION

Your wrists ultimately uncock on the downswing, then recock on the through swing. This uncocking and recocking of your wrists is tied in with rotating the clubface. It's tough to recock if you don't rotate, and rotating is what helps the clubface square up to your target at impact.

If you under-rotate, the clubhead comes into the ball with an open face, which tends to make the ball curve right. If you over-rotate, the clubface comes into the ball closed, which tends to make the ball curve left. A clubface square at impact produces straight shots.

If you swing the club correctly up and around your body, the clubface will rotate somewhat on its own, providing you have a neutral grip. As you swing the club back, the toe of the club works up. As you swing the club through, the toe works up again. The clubface should return to square as you strike the ball.

Of course, sometimes we make mistakes in our swings that throw off this natural rotation and we have to help it along. You can rotate the club in any one of three ways:

• Use a strong grip—in which your hands are rotated more to the right on the club so both "Vs" point beyond your right shoulder—and turn the right hand over the left quickly at impact. Using your hands is an easy way to rotate the clubface but also unreliable because it's difficult to know how much is enough. One time you over-rotate and get a left shot, the next time you under-rotate and get a right shot. You need perfect timing to get predictable ball flight, and we all know timing is just not there every day.

• A more reliable way is to rotate with your forearms. Think left arm over right on the backswing; right arm over left on the through swing. Usually, you must still have a decent pivot to help you rotate

A square clubface at impact tends to make the ball fly straight.

An open clubface at impact tends to make the ball curve right.

A closed clubface at impact tends to make the ball curve left.

your forearms; otherwise, larger muscles will work against the smaller ones, and no matter how much you try to rotate your arms, your body will block you out.

• Concentrate on keeping your hands and arms in front of you and think solely about making a good body pivot. This generally works only for advanced players who overwork their hands and arms. The smaller muscles are going too fast and need calming down.

For most of you, I suggest you key on pivoting and rotating your forearms. Think "Turn and rotate; turn and rotate."

If you are working hard to rotate the clubface but just can't square it up, check your grip first. Next, make sure you are pivoting correctly. If your hips are moving from side to side, your hands and arms will have a hard time rotating because muscles are fighting each other instead of working together.

Now's a good time to review what we've covered and put the big picture back together. Your golf swing is nothing more than a circle. You swing the club up above your right shoulder on the backswing and finish with the club up above your left shoulder. You turn your body back and through, winding up over your right side and then unwinding over your left.

Extending your arms merely keeps your circle big. Cocking and recocking your wrists helps you to rotate the club and square up the clubface at impact. Wrist cock also increases clubhead speed. A good body pivot, a wide circle, wrist cock, and proper club rotation give you distance. The foundation for your circular swing is the good old athletic setup and compatible grip. That's it, ladies!

Concentrate on turning your right forearm over your left as you swing through the ball to help the clubface square up.

HOMEWORK

• Practice for 10 minutes in front of a mirror. Make a few half swings, watching that you keep your triangle intact. Add wrist cock on the backswing and through swing. Feel the club rotate by turning your right forearm over your left before you recock your wrists on the through swing. Make sure you are pivoting as your arms swing up. Picture your swing, then close your eyes and try to feel yourself making the correct swing. Open your eyes and check yourself. Then close them again.

I suggest doing this mirror practice two times a week for as long as you play golf. Seeing, feeling, and knowing you are making the right moves for 10 minutes is better than hitting hundreds of practice balls and hoping you are swinging correctly. If you don't do the above drill regularly, at least do it the night before you have to play.

DRILLS FOR THE PRACTICE TEE

• Warm up.

• Hit 10 balls with a six-iron off a tee. Hit only half shots. Work on swinging the club back and through while keeping your triangle intact. Feel arm extension, pivot, and rotation.

• Hit 10 more half shots with an eight-iron off a tee, maintaining the triangle but now focusing on cocking your wrists. At the top of your half backswing, the grip of the club should point at the ball. At the top of your half through swing, the grip should point to where the ball was. You still must turn your body, even though you're making only half swings. Feel arm extension, wrist cock, pivot, and rotation.

• Using a three-quarter swing, hit 10 balls with a six-iron, thinking about rotating your forearms. Focus only on squaring up the club at impact. Trust the rest of your swing mechanics. Think "Turn and rotate; turn and rotate."

• Now hit five full shots with a six-iron, thinking only of the swing key: turn and stretch; turn and stretch.

• Then hit five full shots with a six-iron, thinking only of the key: turn and cock your wrists; turn and cock your wrists.

• Finish by hitting 10 balls with your six-iron and don't think about anything. Trust your swing and let it all come together.

ARM EXTENSION, WRIST COCK, AND CLUBFACE ROTATION

ARM EXTENSION

- Arms extend at address, and elbows are fairly close together.
- Arms should hang freely at address with little tension.
- Arms create a triangle with your shoulders, and the triangle swings back intact.
- Right arm folds on the backswing; left arm stays extended.
- Both arms are extended just past impact.
- Left arm folds on the through swing; right arm stays extended.
- The more extension, the wider the circle, which means more distance.

WRIST COCK

- Need compatible grip for wrists to cock.
- Strive to cock wrists by the time you've made a three-quarter backswing.
- Pull hands, arms, and club handle down toward the ball, keeping your wrists cocked.
- Re-cock your wrists on your through swing.

CLUBFACE ROTATION

- The clubface rotates toe up.
- The clubface must return to square at impact to prevent major ball flight curve.
- Rotate the clubface either with your hands, forearms, or body pivot.
- For most, it's best to use a combination of forearms and body pivot.

SWING KEYS

"Turn and rotate; turn and rotate."

"Turn and stretch; turn and stretch."

"Turn and cock your wrists; turn and cock your wrists."

"Left over right; right over left."

"Right arm fold; left arm fold."

DAY 4

Grooving Your Swing and Creating Ball Flight

The secret to becoming more consistent is to groove a repeating swing that has few compensating errors. If you always hooked your ball 30 yards or sliced it 20 yards, you could play reasonably good golf. You would know what to expect and could play for it. But when the ball flies right, left, low, or high seemingly at random all in the same round, you've got the proverbial horse of a different color, and the color is trouble. Funny thing is, most of us think we're making entirely different golf swings when we hit all those shots, when in fact our swing hardly changes.

What's happening?

Your natural swing shape is producing a variety of shots, depending on whether the clubface is open or closed at impact, where you strike the ball on the clubface, and how good your timing is. Even with all your new knowledge, you will always have natural tendencies that can creep back into your game and undermine your swing if you're not aware of them. You aren't a machine, and you won't swing perfectly every time. The good news is, you don't have to.

All you really have to do is find out which swing shape is more natural to you and learn what corrections you need to make to get the ball flight you want. That may mean better posture, a different grip, or more body pivot.

SHAPE OF THE SWING

The optimum golf-swing shape is circular, with a fluid motion that works up and around your body on both sides of the ball. The proper blend of up-and-down and around motion gives you the best chance at consistently hitting the ball in the center of the clubface, an important variable to gaining distance and accuracy.

A natural swing shape that's too up and down makes you swing your arms and hands too vertically into the ball and causes "steep misses" like pop-ups, pulls, slices, and topped shots when you lift up, and fat shots when you stay down. With this shape, you'll usually hit a lot of shots off the toe of the club.

To correct this shape, you could round out your swing by either pivoting more or fixing your arm swing. Or you could simply make compensating errors such as strengthening your grip to help you quit slicing, standing closer so the ball won't go off the toe, or aiming more to the left so you can keep your slice in play. You could go on and on. The reality is, a vertical swing and one or more compensating errors will produce some straight shots when your timing is good, but gaining any real predictability is another matter.

A swing shape that's too rounded usually results in hooks, pushes to the right, thin shots, or even shanks, and a lot of balls hit off the heel of your club.

To correct this shape, you could work on swinging your arms more up and down by either cocking your wrists more or swinging the club straighter back from the ball. This might allow your body to pivot more correctly. Or you could choose to compensate by weakening your grip, standing farther away, aiming to the right, etc.

Are you getting the picture? You have a natural swing shape and you can either make a major adjustment to help you swing more up and around or you can choose a "Band-Aid fix" and add a compensating error.

I recommend the lasting fix. Correct your grip, learn to set up athletically and wind up properly, and use your wrists. You've made a good start over the last few days, and your adjustments will hold up better day after day. You may have to review and work a little to change, but it's worth it. After all, Band-Aids do eventually fall off!

In the following photos, the Hula-Hoop simulates a circular golf swing. In the first photo, the swing would be optimum. The Hula-Hoop goes right through the middle of my shoulders and is on a plane that matches the shaft of my club at address. In the second photo, the Hula-Hoop is too vertical compared to my shaft at address. In the third photo, the Hula-Hoop is too rounded.

When your swing shape is correct, you tend to hit straighter shots.

When your swing shape is too vertical, you tend to hit shots off the toe of your club—slices, pulls, fat shots, and tops.

When your swing shape is too rounded, you tend to hit shots off the heel of your club—hooks, pushes, thin shots, and shanks.

FLIGHT OF THE BALL

Naturally, your swing shape affects how your club swings into the ball. Initially, your ball starts out in one of three directions: right of your target, left of your target, or straight at your target. A swing shape that's too up and down produces shots that tend to start to the left. A swing shape that's too rounded produces shots that tend to start right. If you have the proper blend, your shots will start out pretty straight.

Of course, the ball still may curve after it starts out in an initial direction. This curve depends on what the clubface looks like when it strikes the ball. If it's open, the ball tends to curve right. If it's closed, the ball tends to curve left. If it is square, the ball tends to fly straight. The biggest factor affecting the position of the clubface at impact is your grip. After all, your hands are holding onto the club. If you're getting too much curve, check your grip first. Make sure it is not too strong or too weak. Then check your swing shape.

Swing shapes that are too up and down tend to keep the clubface open at impact. Swing shapes that are too rounded tend to close the face too much. Swing shapes with the proper blend tend to keep the face square.

This is starting to sound like *Goldilocks and the Three Bears* and the one that was "just right." Remember, your swing doesn't have to be perfect, but avoid the extremes. A swing shape that's a little too up and down or too rounded will still produce many good shots when your timing is on.

When your swing shape has a good blend of up-and-around motion, you are able to swing the club on a nice arc as you hit your ball. The clubhead actually drops down inside the ball, the face squares up at the ball, then the clubhead travels back to inside of where the ball was. This is an inside-to-inside swing path.

If you try this drill and your clubhead cuts across the arc from outside the first tee and inside the last tee (outside-to-inside swing path), you can bet that your downswing is too vertical. Slices, pulls, and "steep" misses are in your future. It's time to check your pivot fast and stop casting the clubhead from the top. If you can't pivot properly, check your posture and make sure your body isn't in the way.

If you swing inside the first tee and outside the last tee (inside-to-outside swing path), you're probably too rounded. Look out for

When you have the proper blend of up-and-around motion, your club-head swings down on an inside-to-square-to-inside swing path. Your clubhead would pass over all of these tees.

shanks, thin shots, and hooks. You need to swing the club straighter as you take it back and get your arm swing more upright by cocking your wrists more. If you can't, check your grip. Do you see how everything fits together?

As you begin to understand more about why your ball flies as it does, you can begin to fix your swing. You can actually observe your ball flight and try to hit the opposite shot. Oftentimes, by making an exaggerated change the other way, you will get the proper blend of up-and-around motion back quickly. Before you go to the practice tee, glance over the reference sheet on ball flight (page 69). You may want to take it with you to the tee to help you learn to create shots.

HOMEWORK

• Swing a club 50 times in your backyard or inside if you have space. In the beginning, do this in intervals of 10 swings, but work up to doing all 50 at once. Feel your swing repeat. Swing up and around, up and around. Don't be surprised if your best swings come when you are tired and not thinking so much.

• Practice for 10 minutes in front of your mirror. Place quarters on the ground in an arc like the tees in my photo. Practice swinging over the quarters, making an inside-to-inside swing path, with your hands, arms, and body working together. Close your eyes and feel the path. Connect what you saw with what you feel. Now open your eyes and make sure you are still swinging on a good path.

• Face the mirror and tell yourself you are getting better. In fact, you're going to shoot four shots less from now on. It's not that hard. Get your swing to repeat and go out and create ball flight! You now know how to do the full swing. Get it and own it.

DRILLS FOR THE PRACTICE TEE

• Warm up.

• Hit 30 balls off a tee with your eight-iron. Tee up five in a row, leaving about six inches between each ball. Walk up and hit each ball, trying to make exactly the same swing each time. Tee up five

more and continue until you've hit 30 balls. Feel yourself make a
repeating swing.

• Create ball flight with the next 30 balls. Using a five-iron, hit each
ball off a tee so the lie is not a factor. Hit five hooks, five pushes, five
draws, five fades, five slices, and five pulls. Determining which shots
are easiest for you to hit tells you a lot about your natural swing
shape. For instance: To hit an intentional hook, make a very
rounded swing, swinging down on an inside-out swing path, and
close the face at impact. To hit a slice, swing very upright with an
outside-in path on the downswing and keep the clubface open at
impact.

• Hit five more balls, trying to hit the shot most difficult for you.

• Finish by hitting five balls as straight as you can, striving to come
into the ball on an inside-to-inside swing path.

Special Note: I realize we haven't practiced much with woods or
longer irons. You can substitute woods for many of these shots once
you become more proficient. It's easier to groove your swing with
shorter clubs and then adopt that swing for all other full shots. You
just need one swing. The only things that you consciously change as
the club gets longer are (1) you stand farther away from the ball and
(2) you play the ball more forward in your stance.

REFERENCE SHEET: DAY 4

GROOVING YOUR SWING AND CREATING BALL FLIGHT

BALL FLIGHT PATTERNS

Shot Type	Direction Ball Flies	Swing Shape	Downswing Path	Clubface at Impact
Push	Straight right	Too rounded	Swinging to the right (inside to out)	Looking to the right (square to the path)
Hook	Right and curves left	Too rounded	Swinging to the right (inside to out)	Looking left (closed)
Draw	Straight and curves left	Up and around	Swinging down the line (inside to inside)	Looking left (slightly closed)
Fade	Straight and curves right	Up and around	Swinging down the line (inside to inside)	Looking right (slightly open)
Slice	Left and curves right	Too vertical	Swinging to the left (outside to inside)	Looking right (open)
Pull	Straight left	Too vertical	Swinging to the left (outside to inside)	Looking left (square to the path)
Straight	Straight	Up and around	Swinging down the line (inside to inside)	Looking straight (square to the path)

NOTE: *There are always exceptions to the rule. This chart is intended not as absolute, but merely as a guide to get you started in creating ball flight.*

SWING KEY

"Up and around, up and around."

DAY 5

The Putting Grip, Setup, and Stroke

Now that you've got the full swing, get ready. We're going to drop shots fast from here on out. When I say you can easily knock two shots off your score by improving your putting, I'm being modest. You can drop more. Putting accounts for 40 percent of the game, so we've got lots of room to move.

Putting just isn't that hard. It is the shortest stroke, takes the least amount of strength, and requires the fewest moving parts. The lodestar of putting is having a sound stroke you can repeatedly make in the same way time after time after time. With a putting stroke of some predictability, you can acquire feel around the greens. Put the two together and you have a scoring combination.

Many women complain about having no touch on the green. They say they're uncoordinated and not athletic. But, in truth, they just don't have a reliable putting stroke. One time they use wrists; the next time they add weight shift; the next time they stand still. It's virtually impossible to have feel when your stroke is so unpredictable.

So let's get a stroke that works. Memorize it, practice it at home, and trust it when you get to the course. I recommend a putting stroke in which your arms swing from your shoulders and your wrists stay firm. It's the easiest to master because it eliminates excess motion, leaving you only to learn how much swing to make back and through.

But don't get me wrong. There are some excellent wristy putters out there. If you are one, congratulate yourself and just keep working on developing better touch around the greens. If, however, you use wrists and putt erratically—one day good, one day bad—then listen up and try my method.

THE PUTTING GRIP

In the compatible grip you learned on Day 1, you wanted the "Vs" formed by the thumb and forefinger of each hand pointing in the same direction and running parallel to each other. Why? Because this configuration allows your wrists to cock freely. Well, guess what? If you want to restrict any wrist action—and in this putting method we do—simply change your grip so the "Vs" oppose each other.

The most popular putting grip used by good players is the reverse overlap, so why don't you grab your putter and follow along as I describe how it's done.

Place the club handle at an angle across the palm of your left hand and allow it to rest in the second joint of your forefinger. The heel of your hand is more to the side of the grip, rather than on top

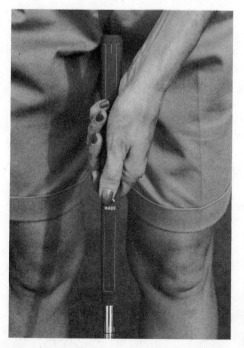

In the putting grip, the club handle rests at an angle in your left hand. The heel pad is to the side of the grip, and the "V" formed with the thumb and forefinger points at your left shoulder.

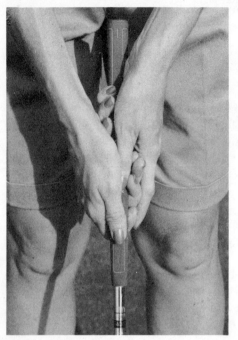

The completed putting grip allows the "Vs" to point to opposing shoulders. Extend your left forefinger over the right fingers to create a reverse overlap grip. Feel the cradle position.

as in the full swing grip, and the thumb-and-forefinger "V" points to your left shoulder. Your left hand will feel much more under the club than it does in your normal grip.

Before placing your right hand on the club, extend your left forefinger straight out to make room. Place the club in your right-hand fingers so the "V" points to your right shoulder. The base of your right hand overlaps the last three fingers of your left hand, and both thumbs rest on top of the putter grip. Now let your left forefinger overlap your right fingers. You can curl it any way that feels comfortable or extend it instead. I like to extend mine. For most putts, use a Level 3 grip pressure, just as in the full swing.

Don't you feel as if you are in a cradling position because of the way your hands are on the club? You should if your grip is correct.

THE PUTTING SETUP

Once your hands are in place, your setup more or less falls into place. Place your feet fairly close together (6–10 inches or wider for long putts), point your toes straight ahead, and keep your feet, hips, and shoulders parallel to your target line. Play the ball up toward your left big toe. If you want to play the ball back more in your stance, that's fine. Just make sure it's ahead of center.

Wherever you play the ball, address it with the center of your putter blade. Many putters have a reminder line on the top of the blade that helps to identify the sweet spot. However, because of manufacturer variances, the line isn't always perfectly placed, but it's close enough.

Bend from the hips so your eyes look almost directly over the ball. (I position mine about two inches inside the ball.) And flex your knees slightly. Your forearms should be in line with the shaft of your putter. Because of your grip and the "cradle position," your elbows point at your hips. Your arms bend slightly and hang freely from your shoulders.

How much your arms bend depends on the length of your putter, your height, and what feels comfortable. If you bend them too much, however, you tend to crouch over the ball, which usually makes you guide the stroke rather than swing the putter. In a correct setup, the arms and shoulders form a triangle from which the putter extends so that your hands are even with the ball at address. This is commonly called a "Y" position.

THE PUTTING STROKE

When you're ready to make the stroke, swing your arms from your shoulders—using no wrist action—and keep the putter blade square to your target line. Your head stays still, your knees stay still, your weight doesn't shift. Concentrate on swinging the "Y" formation back and through. Take care not to let your grip pressure get too tight or you will restrict your arm swing.

To build a repeating, reliable stroke, it's vital to keep the blade square to your target as it swings back and through. Indeed, the blade will appear to open slightly as you swing back, but if you open it too much by allowing the toe of the putter to work back too quickly, you'll have a tough time getting it back to square at impact. The result is usually a missed putt to the right.

If you miss to the right frequently, you'll start aiming to the left to compensate. If that doesn't work, you're liable to use your body to

Bend from the hips so feet, shoulders, and hips are parallel. Elbows point at your hips. Eyes are over the ball or just inside. Note how my forearms are in line with the shaft.

The putter extends from the triangle formed by your arms and shoulders in a way that keeps your hands even with the ball. The ball is positioned forward in your stance. Note the "Y" position.

correct the problem. Do you see how compensations make your stroke erratic? Keeping the blade square throughout the stroke is the source of consistent putting.

The length of the stroke depends on the distance of your putt and the pace of your stroke. Pace is the speed with which you swing your putter, and it should be constant and rhythmic. Think of the pendulum motion of a grandfather clock. It swings tick-tock, tick-tock. It swings back and through the same distance and at the same speed. It doesn't get faster coming through nor does it slow down. This is a good image to keep in mind.

If you feel the inclination to accelerate through a putt, your backswing is probably either too short for the distance at hand or just too slow. A rush coming through the ball leads only to pushed putts to the right and the need for more compensations.

As long as you swing your arms from your shoulders—the keynote of a good stroke—the putterhead swings not only back but up as well. Upon coming down and through in the forward swing, a certain natural acceleration occurs as you strike the ball. There's no need to manufacture it. If your pace is constant, all you need to think about is how much stroke. Keep it simple.

GAUGING THE SPEED

How do you know how much stroke to use? You must experiment.

Begin by recognizing that your personality and the way you do things come into play here. If you're laid-back, you'll probably like a slower pace. If you rush through your day at 80 miles an hour, you're going to like a faster speed. But whichever way your personal traits tend, you'll soon realize that the slower you swing, the longer the stroke you must make, and longer strokes get off track more easily than shorter ones. Equally as troublesome, of course, are fast-paced strokes that get jerky and lack touch. It's a good idea to find a happy medium.

I suggest practicing in ways that help create a rhythmic stroke. You might count as you stroke to music, "One and two, one and two." Or find a word to help suggest the rhythm of your swing. I use "watermelon." "Water" on the backswing and "melon" coming through.

Once you've established your pace, you can focus on the length of your stroke, which depends totally on the distance you want your ball to roll. On short putts, take the blade back a short distance. On medium and long putts, increase the length of your swing accordingly, matching the stroke to the distance. The through swing will always be a little longer than the backswing because of the natural acceleration.

To help solidify your reliable putting stroke, select three distances from which to practice and make them your reference strokes. To groove your short stroke, practice six-footers; for your medium stroke, practice 24-footers; and for your long stroke, practice 45-footers. Always pick flat putts and actually pace off your distances on the practice green and mark them with tees. (A six-footer is two paces if you walk in one-yard strides.) Don't just guess. This really pays off when you play on the course.

HOMEWORK

• Practice your putting grip and setup for five minutes in front of a mirror. Follow the reference sheet and observe the checkpoints listed. Practice with your eyes open, then close them and connect what you see with what you feel. Watch for a quiet body and no wrist action.

• Lay down two clubs parallel to each other to create a putting track. Allowing a one-half to one-quarter inch margin of error between the head of your putter and each club, practice your stroke back and through without touching the clubs. To do so, you'll have to keep the blade square. Turn on some of your favorite music to help you develop pace, but use music without lyrics so you have less distraction. Spend 15 minutes with this drill and begin to develop a repeating stroke.

• Spend three minutes practicing with your head against the wall and your blade against a baseboard in your house. This trains your head and body to remain steady throughout the stroke. (The blade stays square, too.) This drill is especially good after you've practiced putting to music and perhaps have found too much rhythm and started to dance. Remember, to groove a consistent stroke, it's important not to shift your weight or move your head when you putt.

Practice with your putting track to train the blade to stay square. Practicing to music can help develop a constant pace to your stroke.

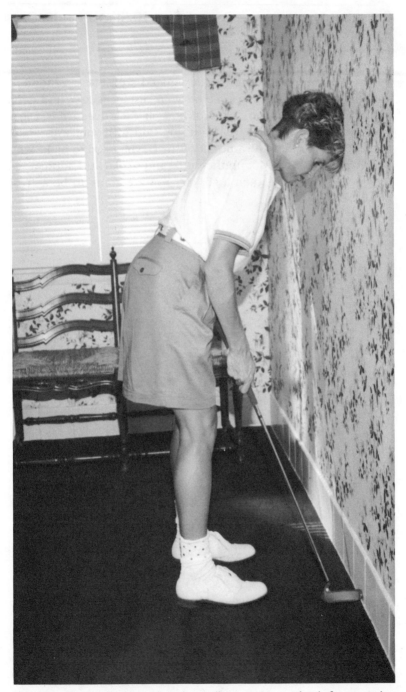

Putting with your head against the wall prevents your body from moving and keeps the blade square.

DRILLS FOR THE PRACTICE GREEN

Spend 30 minutes putting the designated six-footers, 24-footers, and 45-footers. Be sure to pace off your distances first, and get a very clear picture in your mind of how far each distance is. Close your eyes and memorize what you saw. Putt with your eyes open, then closed, and feel the amount of stroke you need to make your ball go the distance. Mix up the putts, and stroke at random a six, then a 24, then a six, then a 45, etc. You are going to be a great putter! Believe it!

REFERENCE SHEET: DAY 5

THE PUTTING GRIP, SETUP, AND STROKE

PUTTING GRIP

- Left-hand "V" formed with thumb and forefinger points at your left shoulder.
- Right-hand "V" formed with thumb and forefinger points at your right shoulder.
- Both thumbs rest on top of the putter grip.
- Left forefinger curls around or extends across right fingers.
- Base of right hand overlaps the last three fingers of the left hand.
- Use a Level 3 grip pressure for most putts.

PUTTING SETUP

- Feet are fairly close together (6–10 inches); toes point straight ahead; weight is even on both feet.
- Feet, hips, and shoulders are parallel to intended target line.
- Ball is positioned toward inside of left foot. Address the ball across from the line on your putter.
- Eyes look over or slightly inside the ball.
- Bend from the hips so arms hang, and flex knees slightly.
- Forearms are in line with shaft; elbows point at your hips.
- Arms are bent slightly.

PUTTING STROKE

- Swing arms from shoulders without using body or wrists.
- Your putter blade should look at your intended target.
- Keep blade square at impact.
- Length of stroke depends on the distance your putt must travel and the pace of your stroke.
- Pace should be constant and rhythmic.
- For very long putts, widen your stance slightly and use a little wrist action.

SWING KEYS

"Swing the 'Y' formation."

"Blade square."

"Watermelon."

"Pendulum on a clock."

DAY 6

Developing Feel and Reading Greens

Developing the kind of feel that brings consistency to your putting game is a twofold proposition. First, you must build a reliable stroke. Second, learn how to make that stroke effective by planning your putts accurately.

You already have the means to satisfy the first requirement. Once your reference strokes are well rehearsed, you're ready to start practicing putts of varying lengths. A 12-footer, for example, is half as much as a 24-footer, so simply find your 24-foot stroke and cut it down. For a 30-footer, find your 24-foot and 45-foot strokes and create something in between. If you have an 18-footer uphill, play it with your 24-foot stroke. Use your imagination and common sense. Before long, you'll have a tangible reference network with which to confidently judge your putts.

The second, more cerebral, requirement is on our plate today. With a reliable putting stroke working for you, you can further develop your feel by learning to read greens. Let's identify just what we're looking for:

• *Slope of the green.* Is the general contour uphill or downhill? Be observant as you walk up to the green and your ball from the fairway. If you have a long putt, walk up to the hole along your estimated target line and feel the slope with your feet, survey it with your eyes. Pace off your putt so you know the exact distance. This way you can use your reference strokes to determine how much swing to make.

• *Condition of the green's grass.* Is it wet or dry? Soft or hard? Long or short? These factors affect the speed of your putt. Wet greens, perhaps obviously, are much slower than dry ones. As greens dry out, they get faster. Remember this for those early-morning tee times. Also, be aware that the practice putting green and the greens on the course are not always the same due to maintenance schedules, so always get a good read on the first green. Generally, the longer the grass, the slower the putts. If the grass is tight to the ground and growing in one direction—a grainy condition— the ball will roll faster with the grain, slower against it.

• *Inhibiting marks.* If ball marks mar your putting line, fix them with a tee or green-repair tool. An unrepaired mark can bump your putt off line or slow it down. Spike marks may also affect your putt, but according to the USGA *Rules of Golf,* you can't fix those before you putt. However, it's a good idea to fix them afterward for players behind you, especially marks close to the hole. This courtesy will keep you in good graces with the golf god, and you're liable to get a lucky break somewhere else on the course.

• *Target line.* The culmination of your reading is deciding on your target line, the line on which you want to start your putt rolling. Stand behind your ball, keeping the hole in front of you, and imagine your ball rolling right up into the cup. Ask yourself which way it will roll. You're looking for a break in the green that would take your ball either right or left. Once you read the break, you'll aim either right or left with both your stance and the putter blade to allow your ball to follow the natural contour of the green and break into or close to the hole.

• Finally, read the green for makable or lag range. I know you've heard the concept about "Never up, never in." Well, it doesn't always apply. Obviously, if you don't get your ball to the hole, it won't go in, but for really long putts your concern is more with making a safe two-putt than going for it in one and ending up with a three-putt. For example, for an uphill putt from 35 feet, your goal is to leave yourself the easiest second putt if the first doesn't go in. Ramming the putt four feet past the hole and leaving yourself a downhill, breaky four-footer is not my idea of an easy putt. Don't do it.

As part of your reading process, label each putt as a *makable* or a *lag.* Your makable range is based on your ability and confidence. It may be five feet or 25 feet—you choose. Certainly, flat, straight putts are easier than double-breakers. You may go for a 15-foot

Bend down behind the ball so you can clearly read your target line. Evaluate break, slope, grass length and type, and any marks on the green between your ball and the hole.

straight putt but lag a 10-foot downhiller. When you lag, estimate the best spot from which to come into the hole on your next putt—right, left, in front of, or behind the hole. Make your plan and do it.

THUMB RULES FOR PUTTING

The best general guideline is to read for speed and distance on long putts and for direction and break on short putts. Of course, that doesn't mean you totally disregard the direction for a 40-foot putt. Just get the general idea of the contour and aim a little right or left as needed; then concentrate on how hard to hit the putt, how much stroke you need.

Women three-putt long putts more often because distance is off, not direction. For short putts, you must be more accurate with your direction because there isn't as much margin for error. If you miss a four-footer because you aimed two feet off line, you've got trouble. Your eyes and feel will generally give you a natural read on distance, so concentrate heavily on the break and where to start your ball out.

Here are other helpful thumb rules:

• If you can't see the break clearly, play your putt straight.

• If the putt breaks in more than one direction, be most aware of how it breaks near the hole. A ball will always be affected by the break more when rolling slowly. You can actually hit a putt through the break if you hit it hard enough, but look out if it doesn't go in the hole.

• Read breaks on long putts from the middle of your putt. For example, if you have a 40-footer, go to the 20-foot mark, bend down, and read the green. If you have a hard time seeing the break, imagine pouring a pitcher of milk between your ball and the hole and observing which way the milk seeps. This visual image tells you what your ball will do. In general, the putt will usually not break as much as it looks.

HOMEWORK

Follow the same homework as for Day 5. Groove your stroke at home so all you have to focus on at the course is developing feel and reading greens.

Go for broke on makable putts. Gauge the speed and direction of your putt and strive to roll the ball right into the back of the cup.

On lag putts, determine the best spot to stroke your first putt toward so you leave yourself an easy second putt.

Drills for the Practice Green

• Play nine holes on the practice green with one ball and read every putt for conditions, slope, distance, length of grass, marks between your ball and the hole, and target line. Keep score and strive to shoot 18 or less.

• Spend 10 minutes putting six-footers, 24-footers, and 45-footers at random to practice your reference strokes. (Pace off your distances and use tees to mark them to ensure accuracy. Don't estimate.)

• Spend 10 minutes putting from a variety of distances, but call the distance before each putt. Putt a five-footer, a 28-footer, a 12-footer, etc. Practice the appropriate reference stroke before you hit each putt.

• Create a ladder drill by placing 10 balls in a line from a cup, with the first ball three feet from the hole and each successive ball three feet farther from the hole. Begin with the first ball—a three-foot putt—and putt each successive ball while concentrating on the length of stroke you need. Your last putt will be from 30 feet. The better you get at this drill, the better your touch will become.

• Finish by putting one ball nine holes on the practice green. Make up your own course. Include three six-footers, three 24-footers, and three 45-footers. Mix up the holes so all the six-footers aren't in a row, and strive to shoot no more than 16. (To be really hard on yourself, repeat the drill if you go over 16 until you shoot your target number.)

Developing Feel and Reading Greens

- The six-foot, 24-foot, and 45-foot putts should become your reference strokes.
- Practice your technique at home so all you work on at the course is developing feel and reading greens.
- Read greens with your eyes and your feet.
- Your reading checklist should include:
- condition of green—wet, dry, slow, fast, cut or uncut, type of grass;
- slope—uphill, downhill, mounds;
- appropriate target line—break right or left;
- marks between your ball and the hole.
- If you can't see the break clearly, play the putt straight.
- If the putt breaks in many directions, be most aware of how it breaks near the hole, where the ball will be rolling the slowest.
- Read the break on long putts from the midway point.
- If you have a hard time seeing the break, imagine pouring a pitcher of milk and seeing which way the milk seeps.
- Focus on speed and distance for long putts, direction and break for short putts.
- Read the putt for makable or lag range; your target may not always be the hole.

Swing Keys

"Never up, never in for makable putts only."

"Read the speed."

"I love to putt, and I'm good at it."

DAY 7

Chipping and Pitching

As we move into the short game, take what you've learned in putting the past two days and bring it along. Reading greens, developing feel, and simple strokes are important for all shots around the green.

The secret to a productive short game is predictability. When you want your ball to run, you want run. When you want it to stop, you want stop. Who needs those holes where you hit two wonderful shots close to the green, then take four more to get your ball in the hole? How can it take two to go 300 yards and four to go 25 yards? Something is wrong with this picture, and we're going to fix it. With some attentive practice, everyone can have an effective short game. Proper setup, good technique, and accurate club selection can be learned. It's a simple matter of memorization.

For our purposes, the short game includes any shot inside of sand-wedge distance that doesn't require a full swing. Because you're not taking a full swing, adjustments must be made in setup, club selection, length of swing, amount of body pivot, and wrist cock.

THE CHIP SHOT

Picture the shot in your mind. The chip is a low-running shot in which the ball stays in the air a short distance—about one-third of its total travel—and then rolls like a putt. Think bowling. It's best used when your ball lies close to the green and has little trouble to clear.

I recommend using three clubs for your chipping. Practice with each of them, know how they react, and make them your weapons! Choose either your pitching wedge, eight-iron, and six-iron, or your nine-, seven-, and five-irons. (I like the first three myself.) Use the most lofted club for short chips and downhill shots, the least lofted for long chips and uphill shots. If you always play on fast, small greens, you may never chip with a six- or five-iron.

As the chip shot usually affords the chance to get your ball close to the hole, read the green just as you do when putting, observing any slope and determining your intended target line. There is no reason why you can't think of chipping in terms of makable and lag ranges as well. Figure out where you want your ball to land and where you want it to end up, then prepare accordingly.

The Setup: Choke down about two inches and grip the club with either your full-swing grip or your putting grip. (You are not going to be using wrists on this shot, so it helps to get your hands in an opposing fashion as in the putting grip to prevent getting "wristy.") Position your feet close together, with your toes pointing straight ahead, and keep your feet, hips, and shoulders all parallel to your intended target line. Play the ball either in the center of your stance or slightly back toward your right foot.

Bend from the hips so your eyes are almost over the ball. You should feel like you're standing very upright because the club is usually longer than your putter. Your arms hang and may even bend slightly. Your grip pressure is Level 3.

Now here's the main key: Your swing center—a point located midway between your sternum and your left armpit—should be positioned left of your ball. Your hands hang below your swing center, so they also should be left of the ball at address. As a result, your weight favors your left foot. This address position encourages you to contact the ball on the downswing, which helps make your ball run. You lean to the left and lead with the left hand because it's in the front.

Remember to always start the lean to the left with your swing center. Too often players lean to the left with their legs but forget to set their upper bodies ahead. With your swing center back, you'll tend to scoop the ball as you strike it, causing you to catch the ball on the upswing, with results worthy of Pandora's box: sculls over the green, fat shots, shots that go too high and stop when you expected

In the chipping setup, your toes point straight ahead and your feet, hips, and shoulders are parallel. You should feel as though you are standing very upright because your eyes are almost over the ball.

Swing center ahead of ball

Your feet are close together, and your ball is in the middle of your stance or slightly back. Note how my swing center, hands, and weight are left of the ball. This setup helps you catch the ball on the downswing.

Swing center behind ball

If you set up with your swing center behind the ball, you'll tend to scoop the ball at impact and run the risk of hitting sculled shots, fat shots, or high shots that don't run when you expect roll.

a low-running shot, and so on. Remember, we're after predict-ability, not random ball flight.

The Stroke: Once your setup is good, the chip stroke is easy. You simply swing your arms back and through. No wrist cock. No weight shift. You don't need them for such a short distance. Keep your stroke simple. Don't use any movement you don't need. Your swing will have very little arc to the inside because you're standing close to the ball with your eyes almost over it, and the length of stroke will be about the same on both sides of the ball. The chip feels a lot like putting with an iron with a lean to the left in the setup.

By leaning even more left with your swing center, hands, and weight or by positioning the ball farther back in your stance, you can make your ball go lower. You could also use a less-lofted club. This is one of the many variations of the basic technique that will blossom through experimentation and practice.

THE PITCH-AND-RUN SHOT

The pitch-and-run shot carries about halfway in the air and rolls the rest of the way. Think tossing. It requires more swing than a chip and, because of its higher trajectory, is best played when you have trouble to clear such as a mound, a bunker, or tall grass. It's also handy when you're close to the green in a chipping situation but have a bad lie. If your ball is sitting down in a hole, you need descent to get the ball up and out no matter how close you are to the green. With the pitch-and-run, you're going to use a little wrist action on your backswing, which means the club will strike the ball with more descent than with the chip. The more descending the strike at impact, the higher the ball flies.

Practice pitch-and-run shots with both a pitching wedge and a sand wedge. Use the pitching wedge when you want more run, face an uphill shot, or have a longer distance to go. Use the sand wedge when you need your ball to stop faster, face a downhill shot, or have a shorter distance to go. Don't let the sand wedge scare you. It's a great club when you learn how to use it.

As with the chip, read the green as you would for a putt, paying close attention to slope and deciding where your ball should land on the green. If you land the ball on an uphill slope, it's going to stop more quickly no matter what technique you use. If the ball lands on a downhill slope, it'll run like crazy, so play for it. Make your plan, decide on your target line and landing area, and prepare.

The Setup: Choke down two inches on the club handle and use your full-swing grip. Since we want some wrist action on the backswing—and therefore need the parallel "Vs" again—don't use your putting grip. Position your feet a little wider than for chipping, and open your stance slightly. Your feet, hips, and shoulders are still parallel to each other but now point slightly left of your intended target line. Your arms hang from your shoulders.

Stand farther from the ball than for chipping to allow for a longer swing. Play the ball in the center of your stance and maintain a Level 3 grip pressure.

Again, your swing center, hands, and weight should be left of the ball at address, although not as much as for the chip shot. You still want to catch the ball on the downswing to get it running after some air time.

The Stroke: The pitch-and-run stroke is a "hinge and hold" technique. You hinge your wrists on the backswing, but use no wrists on the through swing. The backswing is usually longer than the through swing, and you still don't shift your weight on the backswing. Once you're in a good address position, keep your weight left and just swing your arms, using the appropriate wrist action. I suggest you "address for success." That is, set up in the position you want to be in when you strike the ball. You should get some turn through with your body on your forward stroke, especially when hitting a longer shot.

You can create other pitch shots by increasing the amount of wrist action. For example, if your ball is sitting "down," use more wrist action to add descent. For lies sitting up, use only a slight wrist hinge. To achieve a higher trajectory, which will make your ball roll less after landing, lean less to the left or open your clubface. To hit a lower shot with more run, play the ball back in your stance. To hit the ball farther, add more arm swing and body pivot. (If you add body pivot, you'll probably add some wrist action in the through swing.)

Once you understand what makes a ball run and what makes it stop, you open yourself up to the wonderful world of creative shotmaking around the green.

Swing center slightly ahead of ball

In the pitch-and-run setup, your weight, hands, and swing center are slightly left of the ball (but not as far as for the chip). The ball is in the center of your stance.

The pitch-and-run backswing requires some wrist hinge to supply more descent on the downswing. This gets the ball up at the start of the shot.

The pitch-and-run followthrough requires no wrist action for most shots. You "hold" your wrist position instead as your body turns through slightly.

Homework

• Stand in front of your mirror and identify your swing center. Point to it, see it, then close your eyes and feel where it is.

• Practice your chipping and pitching setups and strokes for 10 minutes in front of the mirror. Check yourself in the mirror, then practice with your eyes closed until you can feel what is correct. Feel yourself striking an imaginary ball on the downswing. (No divots in the carpet, please!)

• While still in front of the mirror, alternate setting up for a chip and a pitch-and-run so you can see and feel the difference.

Drills for Near the Practice Green

• Hit 20 chip shots each to a 24-foot target and a 45-foot target. These can become your reference chips. Pace off your distances (no estimates). Try to get each ball within a three- to six-foot circle around the hole.

• Hit 20 pitch-and-run shots each to a 20-yard target and a 40-yard target. Again, more reference strokes, so be sure to pace off your distances. Try to get each ball within a six- to 12-foot circle around the hole.

• Play nine holes around the green with one ball. Begin each hole with your ball off the green and select various lies and distances. After deciding whether you'll play a chip or a pitch-and-run shot, determine which club to use, read the green, and make your plan. Score as low as you can. This enjoyable exercise makes your short-game practice fly by.

REFERENCE SHEET: DAY 7

CHIPPING AND PITCHING

CHECKLIST

Factors	Chip	Pitch-and-Run
Visual image	Bowling	Tossing
Formula	1/3 air time, 2/3 roll	1/2 air time, 1/2 roll
Where to use	Close to the green when you can't putt	Over mounds, trouble, and from bad lies close to the green
Clubs to use	PW, 8, 6 or 9, 7, 5 irons	Pitching or sand wedge
Grip	Putting or full-swing grip (choke down)	Full-swing grip (choke down)
Distance from ball	Stand close	Stand a little farther away
Stance	Square	Slightly open
Ball position	Back or in middle of stance	Middle of stance
Grip pressure	Level 3	Level 3
Swing center/weight	Swing center, hands, weight on left side of ball	Swing center, hands, weight on left side of ball
Wrists	No wrists either side	Wrists on backswing, none on through swing
Angle of approach	Catch ball on downswing	Catch ball on downswing
Length of swing	Backswing and through swing match	Backswing longer than through swing
Pivot	None, preset weight to left	None, preset weight to left (You may pivot more as you hit longer shots)

SWING KEYS

"Lean to the left, lead with the left." (*chip*)

"Hinge and hold." (*pitch*)

"Never use anything you don't need."

"Never play a tough shot when an easy one will do."

"Address for success."

"Predictability."

DAY 8

Lofting Your Ball Over or Out of a Bunker

Adding the high, soft, delicate shot called the lob to your bag of short-game tricks will add another dimension to shotmaking and scoring ability. After mastering the lob, you'll love your sand wedge because of how it can make your golf ball dance. Moreover, with the lob-shot technique as your foundation, your bunker game will flourish.

For lob and bunker shots, the sand wedge steps to center stage. If you look at the bottom of your sand wedge, you'll notice a protruding edge. This is the "flange" and the part of the club that cuts through the grass when you hit a lob or the sand when you hit from a bunker.

If your sand wedge has a particularly large flange, you'll need a very fluffy lie to successfully hit a lob. With a moderate amount of flange, you'll still need a good lie, but it won't have to be as perfect. Sand wedges with large flanges are generally easy to use for short sand shots but tough to hit from fairways. I suggest using a moderately flanged sand wedge because you'll be able to hit both bunker and fairway shots well. For success with the sand wedge, it's critical that you have room for the flange to pass under your ball.

THE LOB SHOT

The lob shot goes up high, comes down softly, and, because of the high trajectory, doesn't roll much when it hits the green. The ball doesn't have much spin on it, it simply goes up and "plops" on the green near the hole (we hope), traveling at least two-thirds of the way in the air.

A sand wedge with a large flange is good out of the sand but difficult to hit off the fairway.

Leading edge

Large flange

Leading edge

Average flange

A sand wedge with an average flange is good out of most bunkers and from the fairway. Stick with this type of wedge.

Use the lob when you need to go up and over an obstacle such as a bunker and have little green to work with. With the clubface open, catch the ball on the downswing so you can cut through the grass. However, if your ball is sitting "down" in the grass with no room for the flange to pass underneath, use a modified version of the pitch-and-run shot: square the clubface, use more wrist action, lean a little left, and catch the ball on the downswing. Your ball may run more, but at least you will clear the trouble. Sometimes we have to compromise to play smart golf.

As with other short-game shots, read the green before you set up for a lob, evaluating the slope and deciding on your landing area. The idea is to hit the shot that leaves you with the easiest possible putt.

The Setup: Use your full-swing grip with one modification. Weaken your right hand on the club by moving it more on top and to the left. Now the "V" formed by your thumb and forefinger points at your chin instead of your shoulder, an adjustment that restricts wrist movement and helps keep the clubface open as it strikes the ball. Choke down about an inch on the club handle and use a Level 2 grip pressure to help slow down your swing.

When you're ready, stand your normal distance from the ball for a sand wedge and open your stance slightly so your feet, hips, and shoulders aim slightly left of your intended target. Play the ball forward in your stance toward your left foot.

Your swing center and hands should be even with or behind the ball, with your weight evenly distributed on both feet. Your clubface is open and lying back to help you get more height on your shot.

The Stroke: The lob stroke is a long arm swing that maintains a slow but constant pace. Backswing and through swing should be of equal length, and you should strike the ball at the bottom of your swing arc or on the upswing—not on the downswing. Your swing center and weight should be even with or behind the ball not only at address, but also at impact.

Because you want to use the full loft of the club to achieve a high trajectory and minimize the ball's roll, you don't want the clubface to close much in the forward swing, and that's why very little body pivot or wrist action is used. Too much pivot, and you'll close the clubface with your body. A wristy swing causes the same problem.

Swing center
even or behind ball

For the lob shot, your weight is evenly distributed on both feet. Ball is forward in your stance. Swing center and hands are even with or behind the ball. Clubface is open to promote a higher trajectory.

Indeed, the lob stroke is an "active" arm swing because, given the open clubface and the absence of any wrist cock or body pivot, your ball just wouldn't go anywhere without it. But "active" doesn't mean "tense." Tension is the lob's worst enemy.

In fact, since you must relax to hit it well, the lob is an excellent shot to practice before you play—especially if you're uptight. Just think "Long and lazy." Practicing the lob can also help you get the timing back in your full swing when it has abandoned you.

The one drawback with the lob is you'll be able to hit it only a certain distance and that depends on your strength. If you have to hit a longer shot, modify the technique by squaring the clubface, using more pivot or wrists, or swinging faster. Of course, by doing so you change the characteristics of the shot. The ball may not fly as high or stop as quickly, but sometimes that's a better sacrifice than stepping back to a pitching wedge. It's tough to hit a soft shot with that club.

THE BUNKER SHOT

With the lob shot in mind, let's go to the beach and add the bunker shot to our bag. It's really not that hard. Most bunker errors are made by players who haven't "addressed for success." The bunker shot is indeed a shot of angles for which setup is everything.

Before considering setup and swing mechanics, form a vivid picture in your mind of the two basic sand swings you'll use. Envision a V-shaped swing for short bunker shots and a U-shaped swing for longer ones. The "V" swing is essentially an arm swing that employs little body pivot; therefore, the club follows a steeper, up-and-down swing path than it would normally. The "U" swing is created by adding body pivot to the "V" swing. In general, a sand shot should travel about two-thirds of its total distance in the air and roll the rest of the way.

To minimize frustration and fix the spotlight on your progress, prioritize your goals for bunker shots:

1. Get the ball out of the bunker.
2. Get the ball on the green.
3. Get the ball close to the hole.
4. Get the ball into the hole.

Stick with goals one and two for a while. If you can consistently achieve both in one shot, you'll melt shots off your score. You don't have to be a great bunker player, just a decent one. In fact, the best players in the world get the ball out of the sand and one-putt only 50 percent of the time, and they play this game for a living. If you start moving toward goals three and four, you might look for a new career in golf.

The Setup: When preparing for a sand-wedge shot, enter the bunker from the lowest lip, for safety's sake, and begin to take your stance. After observing your lie, nestle your feet into the sand so you are set slightly lower than the ball, and choke down on the club handle so your clubhead is measured to pass just under the ball. If you dig in too much with your feet, you'll take too much sand on the shot. Choke down too much, and you'll hit the shot thin, contacting the ball and not the sand. It's a matter of being "measured" so that when you swing, the flange strikes the sand, and the sand carries the ball out of the bunker. The club never touches the ball.

Use your full-swing grip with a weaker right-hand position, just as you did for the lob shot, to help keep the clubface open. Read your green as well as what's around the green. Sometimes you may need to aim for the middle of the green to give yourself a bigger landing area or to avoid a large lip on the bunker. Consequently, your intended target line isn't always in line with the hole. Keep your imagination alert.

After determining your target line, assume an open stance by setting your feet, hips, and shoulders on an angle pointing left of your target. Play the ball off your left heel, position your swing center and hands even with or behind the ball, and maintain a Level 3 grip pressure. By leaning left a little with your legs only—not your swing center—your weight can favor your left side. This sets you up to "scoop" a little at impact, but that's all right for bunker shots.

The Stroke: With your setup well measured, stance aimed left, and clubface open, all you do now is swing along your foot line and watch the ball fly toward your target. Allow your wrists to hinge slightly as you swing your arms. The flange is what hits the sand, not the leading edge. If the leading edge strikes the sand first, you'll dig too much and often leave your ball in the sand.

Short bunker shots require little body pivot, but for longer bun-

Swing center behind or even with ball

In the bunker shot, play the ball off your left foot. Your stance is open and aimed to the left. Your swing center and hands are even with or behind the ball. Your clubface is open for short shots and square for longer bunker shots.

ker shots, add pivot to create the U-shaped swing. Remember, pivot gives you power. Add it as you need it. For particularly long bunker shots, add pivot, keep your clubface more square, and use your pitching wedge.

Don't be too concerned if you have trouble with sand shots. As your fundamentals improve, so will your bunker play. In the meantime, compensate by using the pitch-and-run technique out of the bunker and strike your shots more cleanly, not taking so much sand. The ball won't fly as high and will run more, but these are acceptable trade-offs because you can usually get the ball out (goal number one). Just remember to pick a large part of the green to aim toward to allow for the added roll. For buried lies in the bunker, the pitch-and-run technique is ideal.

HOMEWORK

• Practice address positions for the lob shot, greenside bunker shot, and fairway-bunker shot in front of your mirror for 10 minutes. Observe yourself from both the face-on and down-the-line angles. You know the routine. Do it with your eyes open and then closed to get the feel. Always come back to the mirror to check your setups if you have trouble at the course.

DRILLS FOR THE PRACTICE TEE1

• Warm up.

• Make 20 lob-shot swings outside a bunker before ever striking a ball. Feel the long and lazy swing. Find your slower-paced arm swing.

• Select two distances—one about 15 yards and one about 30 yards—and hit 15 lob shots to a target from each spot. Pace off your distance as best you can so you get the feel for the swing length you need to make the ball go different distances. Make these your lob reference strokes.

• Move into the bunker and hit 15 short bunker shots at a target. Then hit 15 longer bunker shots, remembering to square the clubface and add body pivot. If you have trouble getting the ball out, try the following: (1) With a club, draw lines in the sand along your

Notice how my feet, shoulders, and hips aim left of my intended target line. (My target line is to the right of the hole because I'm playing for the slope in the green.) Play the short bunker shot with an open clubface. Swing the club along your foot line and remember to stay measured.

foot line and target line and make sure your stance isn't too open. (2) Draw a circle about the size of a softball where your ball should be. With practice swings, try to remove the circle of sand without hitting a ball. Then put a ball in the circle and continue to practice taking the circle out. Now the ball should come out with the sand. Once you've got it, hit the ball out without drawing a circle.

• Practice five pitch-and-run shots out of a bunker, choosing marginal lies from which to practice.

• Hit 10 fairway-bunker shots back onto the range, using the proper technique.

LOFTING YOUR BALL OVER OR OUT OF A BUNKER

CHECKLIST

Factors	Lob Shot	Bunker Shot
Visual image	"Plop shot"	"V" Shot or "U" shot
Formula	⅔ air time, ⅓ roll	⅔ air time, ⅓ roll
Where to use	To get the ball up fast and make it stop, from a good lie	Bunker or fluffy lie outside bunker
Club to use	Sand wedge	Sand wedge
Grip	Full swing, weak right hand	Full swing, weak right hand
Distance to stand from ball	Same as for sand wedge	Same as for sand wedge
Stance	Slightly open	Slightly open
Ball position	Forward in stance	Off left heel
Clubface	Open	Open for short, more square for long shots
Grip pressure	Level 2	Level 3
Swing center, hands, weight	Behind or even with the ball	Behind or even with the ball (Your leg may lean a little left)
Wrists	A little	More wrists
Angle of approach	Catch ball at the bottom of the arc or on upswing	Catch ball at the bottom of the arc or on upswing
Length of swing	Long arm swing, matching on both sides	Long arm swing, matching on both sides
Pivot	Depends on length of the shot	Add pivot for longer shots

SWING KEYS

"Address for success."

"Long and lazy arm swing." (*lob*)

"Swing down your foot line." (*bunker*)

DAY 9

Short-Game Strategy and Trouble Shots

The purpose of the short game is to get the ball close to the hole. With the chip, pitch-and-run, and lob shots in your short-game shotmaking bag, you've got options for just how to do that. You're not limited to one shot from every situation. As you experiment with variations of the three techniques, you'll add more shots to your repertoire, creating even more options. But keep it simple in the beginning.

Success with short-game strokes—and full-swing strokes as well—depends on the economy of motion in your swing. The fewer moving parts, the less susceptible you are to breakdown, and the more consistent the results.

If you can putt the ball, even when off the green, putt it. If you're a little too far away or the grass between the ball and the green is too thick, that's the time to chip. Chipping is a little tougher than putting because it involves more stroke and, therefore, more body movement. Adhere to the adage "Never play a tougher shot when an easier one will do," which, for short-game shots, means keep your ball as close to the ground as possible and use only the body movement necessary. In other words, putt if you can, chip if you can't putt, pitch if you can't chip, lob if you must.

Working strategy into planning your shot is essentially a three-tiered adventure:

• *Figure your options.* The process begins as you approach your ball near the green and assess your lie, the location of the hole, and any trouble between your ball and the hole. If your lie is bad, you know you can eliminate the lob shot and play either a chip or a pitch-and-run. If you have lots of trouble to clear, you won't play a chip because you'll want the ball in the air longer. If your lie is good, you might play a lob; if marginal, play a pitch-and-run.

• *Connect with your target.* If your mechanical skills are sound and well played, the success or failure of any particular shot depends on how deft you are at selecting a target line on which to hit your ball. Whether you draw an imaginary line in your mind or just feel it, you want to connect with your target and understand how your ball must travel to end up close to the hole.

• *Make your play.* Make your shot and club selection and determine where you want your ball to land by using the formulas—one-third air time for a chip, one-half for a pitch-and-run, and two-thirds for a lob—to decide on a spot. Make your adjustments for any slope of the green. Focus on your spot and execute the shot.

UNEVEN LIES

Expand your strategizing to longer-range shots by learning to play from uneven lies, the source of most "trouble shots." Uphill, downhill, ball-above-your-feet, and ball-below-your-feet lies won't be the only uneven lies you'll come across on the course, but after learning the setups for these four, you can combine techniques and create setups for other uneven lies.

Uphill lie: The main concept to remember is to level out the lie as much as possible. That means setting up with the slope. For the uphill shot, let gravity take you and slant your shoulders with the slope. Play the ball off your high foot (the left) and swing with the slope. Your weight may favor your left side to maintain balance, but your swing center stays back. The ball will fly higher than normal because you effectively add loft to the actual clubface as you swing up the slope. You may want to take more club to make up for this.

Because of the added height, your ball doesn't roll as much. It also tends to fly to the left because your arms and hands can easily pass your body in the swing due to gravity and the slope. Aim a little right to compensate. Use this technique out of bunkers or anywhere else on the course when you have an uphill lie.

To hit the uphill-lie shot, slant your shoulders with the slope and lean into it with your legs for balance. Play the ball off your high foot and swing with the slope. The ball tends to fly higher and to the left, so use more club if necessary, especially for longer shots, and aim right to compensate.

Downhill lie: For the downhill shot, simply reverse your uphill positions. Slant your shoulders down along the same angle as the slope, play the ball off your high foot (the right), let your weight favor the left side because of gravity, and swing with the slope. Hinge your wrists up on the backswing and extend your arms down the slope on the through swing. The ball will fly lower than normal and go slightly right, so use a more lofted club and aim a little left. It'll also roll more, so adjust your landing area.

To hit the downhill shot, slant your shoulders down the slope, play the ball off your right foot, lean with the slope, and swing down it. The ball tends to fly lower, roll more, and go a little right, so compensate accordingly.

Ball above feet: The ball-above-your-feet shot is a lot like playing baseball. Because the ball is closer to you, choke down on the club handle, widen your stance, and flex your knees more than usual. With the ball positioned in the center of your stance, make a very rounded arm swing around your body and contact the ball. Remember, rounded swings tend to make the clubface close, so the ball usually flies left. Aim a little to the right of your intended target.

Ball below feet: When the ball is below your feet, widen your stance a little and bend more from your hips. Don't choke down on the club; the ball is farther away from you and you need all the length you can get. Swing the club on a more up-and-down path, adding wrist cock to help you get down to the ball. The ball will fly right as it comes off this lie, so change your aim. Remember, the ball usually flies with the slope. Balls below your feet curve right; balls above your feet curve left.

As you try these techniques, you may notice that certain shots are easier for you than others. That's because of your natural swing shape. For instance, if your swing is more rounded, you'll like the ball-above-your-feet shot. But that doesn't mean you can't learn the other shots. You just need to know the proper setups and adjustments to make.

Memorize these setups from the reference sheet at the end of this chapter. If you get confused on the course, make practice swings from a lie similar to the one your ball rests in. Watch where your club bottoms out and note how much descent you make when you swing. This will give you a good indication of the adjustments you should make.

HOMEWORK

• Practice your trouble-shot setups in front of a mirror for 10 minutes and observe the differences among them. Look from both the face-on and down-the-line views. You may need to stand on an inclined board to really simulate the various lies. (Those aerobic steps work well if you have one.)

DRILLS FOR THE COURSE:

• Warm up.

To hit a ball above your feet, choke down on the grip, widen your stance, flex your knees more than normal, and make a rounded baseball-type swing. Aim right because the ball tends to fly left.

To hit a ball below your feet, bend over more than usual, don't choke down on the club, and swing your arms more up and down. The ball tends to fly right, so aim left.

• Hit 10 shots each from a downhill, uphill, ball-above-your-feet, and ball-below-your-feet lie. Check the direction and trajectory of each shot.

• Take 30 balls and walk around the green dropping three balls each in 10 different situations. Select chips, pitch-and-runs, lobs, and bunker shots and play the "course." As you come to each new situation, evaluate the lie and what's between your ball and the hole. Go through your procedures and select a club and the shot to play. Experiment. If you try a lob and it doesn't work, try the pitch-and-run. Putt out each ball and see how many up-and-downs you score.

SHORT-GAME STRATEGY AND TROUBLE SHOTS

UPHILL LIE

- Slant shoulders up the slope
- Play ball off left foot
- Weight favors left side for balance
- Ball flies higher, rolls less
- Take more club
- Aim slightly right
- Swing arms up the slope

DOWNHILL LIE

- Slant shoulders down the slope
- Play ball off right foot
- Weight favors left side due to gravity
- Ball flies lower, rolls more
- Take less club
- Aim slightly left
- Swing arms down the slope

BALL ABOVE FEET

- Choke down on club
- Bend over, widen stance, flex knees
- Ball in center of stance
- Round out your arm swing
- Ball will fly left, so aim right

BALL BELOW FEET

- Do not choke down on club
- Bend over, widen stance, flex knees
- Ball in center of stance
- Make a more up-and-down arm swing
- Ball will fly right, so aim left

SWING KEYS

"Focus on your spot and execute the shot."

"Cock wrists up when the ball sits down."

DAY 10

Master Your Pre-Shot Routine and Play Smart Golf

Well, there you have it. Just about all the swing technique you need to drop shots off your score. More will come off as you learn to play smarter golf. Smart golf comes from being prepared, and that's where your pre-shot routine comes in.

"Addressing for success" involves more than just walking up to your ball and hitting your shot at random. You must gather information pertinent to your shot, then proceed in a routine that is the same for putting, chipping, and a full swing. Your routine should be your own and bear your mark, just as long as it includes the essentials of gripping the club, aligning the clubface behind the ball in line with the target, and taking your stance. Grip, clubface, stance. Say it, memorize it, own it.

Keep in mind that your entire pre-shot routine—from the time you begin to gather information to the time you hit your shot—should last no more than 40 seconds. You don't have to be a slow player to be prepared; you just need to be organized. A good pre-shot routine directs your concentration and helps you stay focused under pressure. Your confidence will soar as your scores go down.

Follow me in creating the routine below, which describes what tasks you should include and suggests where to do them. From there, you can add whatever you like. Begin by forming two imaginary boxes from which to play: a "think box," which should be located behind your ball so you can clearly decide on your target; and a "play box," located around where you will actually hit the ball. It's like a baseball game where you see the next batter in the on-deck circle (the think box) preparing her strategy and loosening up. When in the batter's box (the play box), she's ready to swing the bat.

THE THINK BOX

In your think box, you gather information, select your club, get your swing key, grip the club, tell yourself you've got it, and start toward your play box.

• Consider your lie, the wind, how heavy the air is, where the trouble is, and where your best landing area is. Imagine what your ball should look like in flight, and decide what your target should be.

• Select a club that will help you hit your ball toward that target on the appropriate trajectory. Make a practice swing physically or, if you can visualize the shot so clearly, in your mind. If necessary, lodge one swing key in your mind to help keep you on track as you take your practice swing. This swing, whether physical or mental, should be a rehearsal for the shot you are about to perform.

• Grip the club for the practice swing just as you will when you actually hit your shot. It's a good idea to grip in your think box because you can focus on your hands and make sure the clubface is square like we did on Day 1. If you grip the club after setting the clubface down, you're likely to twist the face as you mold your hands on the club. And we sure don't want to start with an error for which we have to compensate later on.

• Finally—and this is huge!—tell yourself you've "got it" before stepping out of the think box. Don't go into your play box with indecision or doubt. Make a plan and stick to it. You may not always execute your plan perfectly, but at least you'll give yourself the best chance.

THE PLAY BOX

Once in your play box, focus totally on your target and the extended line along which you want your ball to fly. Engage your target, align your clubface, take your stance, and hit your shot. You may make your practice swing here if you choose, and if you're good at visualizing how and where the ball should fly, you may also want to select an intermediate target to help your aim. This intermediate target—a blade of grass, a ball mark, or whatever—should be about two feet in front of your ball and in line with your target line.

• You may be able to engage your target just by looking at it and feeling what it will be like to hit the ball streaking toward it, and that feeling might be all you need to execute a great shot. On the other hand, you may need to look at the target and waggle the club a few times to get the rhythm of the swing you need to hit your ball on line. It may be a sense of timing or cadence that makes you engage with your target.

• Whatever your method, the purpose is to get in tune with your target. Don't think of mechanics in your play box, but rather trust your swing no matter what level of player you are. Remember, your swing doesn't have to be perfect. Just get the general circular motion and go with it. You can work on refining mechanics on the practice tee or at home in front of the mirror. When you're on the course, you need to play golf. And that doesn't mean just hitting shots. You put the whole package together. You make a plan. You hit the ball, find it, and you hit it again, striving always to get the ball in the hole in the fewest strokes possible, no matter how pretty or how lucky your shots are.

• After zeroing in on your target, set the clubface down behind the ball in line with your intended target line. Take your stance. Look at your target again to confirm that your alignment will allow your ball to fly to your target. Then swing.

• Watch the flight of the ball. If you hit the shot you wanted, pat yourself on the back. If you missed it, make a quick evaluation of what you could have done better, make a practice swing with the correction, and leave the error right there. (Remember to always keep pace with the group behind you, so this procedure must be fast. If you have no time, make this corrective swing mentally.) Tell yourself your swing is fixed and go on. If you have no idea what you did wrong, go back to your fundamentals. Later, after the round, you can check your reference sheets for help.

You see, your mind is a magical thing. It's really a matter of believing. If you believe your swing is fixed, chances are you will perform well from then on. If you believe you're swinging poorly and you can't hit any ball straight, you probably won't. In golf, you kind of get what you ask for. So from here on out, think a good game and talk a good game, no matter how well you play.

CONCENTRATION

Planning and executing a golf shot takes a good dose of concentration, but no one can concentrate for an entire round of 18 holes without being mentally exhausted when finished. More good news: you don't have to. Think of playing golf down a railroad track. On one side of the track, be yourself. Socialize, if you like, dream, take in the scenery, whatever you enjoy doing on the course. Just stay relaxed and comfortable.

Once you get about 20 yards from your ball, "cross" to the other side of the tracks and go into your pre-shot routine. Here's where you concentrate. Zone in and hit your shot. Give yourself that 40 seconds. Stay with your routine so you're not distracted, and finish your shot. Enjoy the results or make your corrective practice swing, then cross back over the tracks, back into "your world" on the course until you get 20 yards from your next shot, when you'll cross the tracks again.

On and around the green, this sequence quickens. You won't have as much time between shots, but you can still alternate your focus. Concentrate when necessary; give your mind a break when you have the chance. Just be ready to hit when it's your turn.

Directed concentration and a good pre-shot routine will make you a smarter golfer, but you'll need creativity and common sense on the course as well. Accept your poor shots. Inevitably, there will be some. After an errant shot, find your ball, hit it back into play, and go on. Never let one bad shot cost you another. Control your frustrations and play a risky shot only when the odds are in your favor. It's pretty tough to hit woods out of fairway bunkers, especially when there is a lip. It's also tough to hit long irons out of heavy rough. Just take your lumps. Use a more lofted club and set yourself up in front of the green. You're more likely to hit a miraculous shot with a wedge than with a long club.

In your think box, gather information, select your club, get your swing key, grip the club, and tell yourself you've got it.

In your play box, engage your target, position the clubface in line with your intended target line, take your stance, and swing. Enjoy the shot or make a corrective practice swing on the spot.

PLAYING SMART, STAYING HAPPY

Playing smart golf means, in part, playing to your strengths. Experiment with different strategies and find those that rely on the best elements of your game. Experiment, too, in discovering what the best elements of your game are right now.

Consider, for example, using your three-wood more often off the tee instead of the driver. A well-struck three-wood goes farther than a poorly hit driver any day of the week, and the three-wood is easier to hit because it has more loft. Your ball won't curve as much off line because loft helps keep your ball on line. Don't let your peers talk you into a driver just because that's the club you are "supposed" to use. Use the club that helps you hit your target area, whether it's a three-wood or even a five-wood. If what they say bothers you, get a driver made up with three-wood loft and shine above them.

Also, use the five-wood in the fairway instead of the three-wood, especially in the off-season when most courses aren't as lush. I can't tell you how many players come to me and say their swing is gone and they can't hit their three-wood anymore. The problem isn't with them; the lies have gotten worse. You need a pretty plush lie to hit a successful three-wood shot. Using a five- or six-wood is much easier.

Above all, stay light on the course. Laugh, think happy thoughts, and stay in a good frame of mind. You'll play better golf and have more energy when you finish. Register as many good shots as you can in your mind, just like filling up your bank account with big deposits. The more you add, the better you feel. The more negative thoughts you have, the more you withdraw. Walk away from a bad score with a positive outlook and you're likely to have many more good days to follow. Remember, the golf god is always watching!

HOMEWORK

• Practice your pre-shot routine in front of a mirror for five minutes. See what it looks like, then check yourself. Make sure it takes no more than 40 seconds.

DRILLS FOR THE PRACTICE TEE

• Warm up.

• Decide on your pre-shot routine. Experiment with the framework given above and personalize it. Think "Grip, clubface, stance."

• Hit 30 short-game shots from various lies, using your pre-shot routine for every shot.

• Hit 30 full-swing shots using at least three different clubs, and follow your pre-shot routine for every shot. Always aim at a target.

• Practice putting for 15 minutes, using your pre-shot routine. Do some drills, then putt a nine-hole course on the putting green.

MASTER YOUR PRE-SHOT ROUTINE AND
PLAY SMART GOLF

- Keep your pre-shot routine the same for putting, chipping, and the full swing.
- It should last no more than 40 seconds.
- The basic framework includes grip, clubface, stance.
- Use a think box to gather information, select your club, get your swing key, grip the club, and tell yourself you've got it.
- The think box is located behind your ball so you can clearly decide on your target.
- Use a play box to engage your target, set the clubface down in line with your target line, take your stance, and swing.
- Make a corrective practice swing following the shot if you didn't execute it according to your plan.
- Play golf on the railroad tracks, so you concentrate only when you are zoned in.
- Consider hitting more three-woods off the tee and more five-woods off the fairway.
- Stay light; think positively.

SWING KEYS

"Grip, clubface, stance."

"Engage with your target."

"Hit your ball, find it, and hit it again."

"Get your ball in the hole in the fewest strokes possible."

"Never let one bad shot cost you another."

DAY 11

The 40-Minute Practice Program and Keeping Score

As you continue to think your way to lower scores, it's important to measure your progress. You need to set goals, perform, and evaluate. Make improving a game. Every time you break your scoring record or knock shots off your short game five rounds in a row, celebrate. You deserve it. Don't turn improving at golf into another job.

Short-term goals let you taste progress on an ongoing basis. You can achieve your plan, pat yourself on the back, then set a new goal. Here are some sample short-term goals:

- Average 34 putts per 18 holes for the next 10 rounds of golf. If you play nine holes, shoot for 17.
- Hit 70 percent of the fairways over the next 10 rounds. That's about 10 of 14 on a regulation course.
- Get every bunker shot out of the sand trap on the first attempt.
- Get 80 percent of your chips and pitch-and-run shots down in three shots or less.

Whatever short-term goals you choose, make them attainable. Write them down and carry them with you to the course when you play or practice. Don't hit balls on the practice range without a purpose. I'd much rather hit fewer balls while trying to reach a goal than beat balls at random.

Long-term goals help keep your "whole game" in perspective.

You observe the ebb and flow of your game over long periods of time and come to know your strengths and weaknesses well. In time, you become a very good judge of where your game is and where you need to take it.

• Lower your handicap by five shots over the next six months. That doesn't mean taking off 10 shots from just one round of golf, but rather shooting five to 10 shots lower every time you play—the sort of self-challenge that brings out your best.

• Play golf at least once a week for the next six months. Playing regularly can only help you improve because we learn the most by doing. I can teach you all the technique in the world, but you won't "get it" until you experience it for yourself. Find a regular playing partner or consider joining one of the women's golf leagues that are becoming more and more popular every day.

• Set a long-term goal to play in a golf tournament at your club, in the city, or on the state level. This requires you to make a plan so you're prepared when the event arrives. Include some intangible goals such as having more fun playing golf and coming off the course smiling. I guarantee you'll play and practice more if you have fun doing it. Whatever your goals may be, set them, achieve them, then set new ones.

A GOOD 40 MINUTES

Setting goals is the easy part. Achieving them is the heart of the matter. The structured, 40-minute practice program outlined in the charts on the following pages will help you get to the heart. Tailored to four different handicap levels, the program is filled with built-in goals. Some are easy to reach, some more challenging. Start and stick with the program that meets your current ability. As you improve, set a goal to meet the requirements of a lower handicap golfer and keep progressing.

The program calls for hitting a variety of shots that are common on the course, plus includes time for "creative shotmaking," in which you practice from unusual but not unheard-of lies. Look for uneven lies, different obstacles to carry, different lengths of grasses, trees to hit around, and whatever you can imagine.

Think carefully about what club to use and the trajectory you want your ball to fly on. Experiment. If you hit a shot only one time in practice, you'll be that much better at it on the course. Your imagination will catch fire, and that, my friends, is what you need to drop strokes off your score. Keep in mind: Practice like you play and you'll play like you practice.

KNOW YOUR TARGETS

In the program charts that follow, you'll find specific targets given for short-game and putting practice. Be fairly precise in measuring your targets to help sharpen your accuracy. Anything right, left, short, or long inside four feet is good. Pat yourself on the back! The targets for the full swing are a little more vague because not all practice tees have flags and greens to hit to. You're going to have to use your imagination, but it's easy. Just use common sense. Here are some hints:

• For short approach shots with wedges, you want to get the ball close to the hole. In practice, aim at an imaginary green (or circle within a green) that's about 30 feet in diameter. If you're a 10-handicap player or better, make your circle even smaller and expect to hit each shot within 20 feet to give you lots of birdie and "save par" opportunities.

• For medium approach shots with the five-, six-, or seven-iron, make your imaginary green approximately 30 yards in diameter, a common green size. If you're a 10-handicapper or better and want to aim for a smaller green, go for it. The better you do in practice, the lower the scores you can expect on the course.

• For long approach shots with the three- or four-iron or fairway woods, again aim at your 30-yard green. High-handicappers won't hit many greens from this distance, but that's expected. The key is getting your mis-hits as close to the green as possible. Missing the green by 10 yards is better than missing it by 20. Hit as many shots as you can on or near the green and keep the others in play. Even if they don't get up in the air or feel great when you hit them, it doesn't matter. As long as you advance toward your target with reasonable distance, you can lower your scores.

• For tee shots, aim toward a typical fairway width—about 40 yards. If possible, pick two landmarks to aim between to better simulate a fairway. Your goal is to keep your ball in the fairway, but if it goes out, you want to be close. The shots to eliminate, of course, are the ones that go way off line, the ones that find the water hazards or deep woods, the ones that make your scores soar. It's usually not the occasional topped shot or worm burner that costs you a good score.

As you practice tee shots, if you can't keep a driver in the fairway zone, drop back to your three- or five-wood and see how you do. Find a club that you can keep in play and use that club on the course. Your score will improve. I could break 80 before I ever owned a driver. Don't pressure yourself into hitting the driver before you're ready.

Here's how the program lays out. Just find your handicap and study your chart:

Players with Handicap Levels of 30-plus

What to Practice	How Long	Distance	Club to Use	No. of Balls	Goal
Full swing	15 minutes	Short approach	Wedge	10	30%
		Medium approach	7, 6, 5-iron	10	20%
		Long approach	4, 3-iron or fairway wood	10	10%
		Tee shot	Driving club	10	50%
Chip	3 minutes	25 feet	Pitching wedge	5	1 in 4-ft. circle 2 in 8-ft. circle 2 on green
		45 feet	8-iron	5	1 in 4-ft. circle 1 in 8-ft. circle 3 on green
Pitch	5 minutes	20-yard pitch-and-run	Pitching wedge or sand wedge	5	2 in 8-ft. circle 3 on green
		30-yard lob shot	Sand wedge	5	1 in 8-ft. circle 4 on green
Bunker	5 minutes	20-yard short bunker	Sand wedge	5	1 in 8-ft. circle 4 on green
		40-yard long bunker	Sand wedge	5	5 on green
Putt	7 minutes	3 feet	Putter	8	Make 4
		24 feet	Putter	8	5 in 4-ft. circle
		45 feet	Putter	8	2 in 4-ft. circle 4 in 8-ft. circle 2 miss circles
Creative shotmaking	5 minutes	You select	You select	5	You decide

PLAYERS WITH HANDICAP LEVELS OF 20–29

What to Practice	How Long	Distance	Club to Use	No. of Balls	Goal
Full swing	15 minutes	Short approach	Wedge	10	60%
		Medium approach	7, 6, 5-iron	10	30%
		Long approach	4, 3-iron or fairway wood	10	20%
		Tee shot	Driving club	10	60%
Chip	3 minutes	25 feet	Pitching wedge	5	3 in 4-ft. circle 2 in 8-ft. circle
		45 feet	8-iron	5	2 in 4-ft. circle 3 in 8-ft. circle
Pitch	5 minutes	20-yard pitch-and-run shot	Pitching wedge or sand wedge	5	5 in 8-ft. circle
		30-yard lob shot	Sand wedge	5	3 in 8-ft. circle 2 on green
Bunker	5 minutes	20-yard short bunker	Sand wedge	5	1 in 4-ft. circle 3 in 8-ft. circle 1 on green
		40-yard long bunker	Sand wedge	5	5 on green
Putt	7 minutes	3 feet	Putter	8	Make 5
		24 feet	Putter	8	6 in 4-ft. circle
		45 feet	Putter	8	3 in 4-ft. circle 5 in 8-ft. circle
Creative shotmaking	5 minutes	You select	You select	5	You decide

PLAYERS WITH HANDICAP LEVELS OF 10-19

What to Practice	How Long	Distance	Club to Use	No. of Balls	Goal
Full swing	15 minutes	Short approach	Wedge	10	60%
		Medium approach	7, 6, 5-iron	10	50%
		Long approach	4, 3-iron, or fairway wood	10	30%
		Tee shot	Driving club	10	70%
Chip	3 minutes	25 feet	Pitching wedge	5	4 in 4-ft. circle 1 in 8-ft. circle
		45 feet	8-iron	5	3 in 4-ft. circle 2 in 8-ft. circle
Pitch	5 minutes	20-yard pitch-and-run shot	Pitching wedge or sand wedge	5	2 in 4-ft. circle 3 in 8-ft. circle
		30-yard lob pitch	Sand wedge	5	1 in 4-ft. circle 4 in 8-ft. circle
Bunker	5 minutes	20-yard short bunker	Sand wedge	5	2 in 4-ft. circle 3 in 8-ft. circle
		40-yard long bunker	Sand wedge	5	1 in 8-ft. circle 4 on green
Putt	7 minutes	3 feet	Putter	8	Make 6
		24 feet	Putter	8	8 in 4-ft. circle
		45 feet	Putter	8	2 in 4-ft. circle 3 in 8-ft. circle
Creative shotmaking	5 minutes	You select	You select	5	You decide

PLAYERS WITH HANDICAP LEVELS OF 0-9

What to Practice	How Long	Distance	Club to Use	No. of Balls	Goal
Full swing	15 minutes	Short approach	Wedge	10	80%
		Medium approach	7, 6, or 5-iron	10	50%
		Long approach	4, 3-iron, or fairway wood	10	40%
		Tee shot	Driving club	10	70%
Chip	3 minutes	25 feet	Pitching wedge	5	5 in 4-ft. circle
		45 feet	8-iron	5	3 in 4-ft. circle 2 in 8-ft. circle
Pitch	5 minutes	20-yard pitch-and-run shot	Pitching wedge or sand wedge	5	2 in 4-ft. circle 3 in 8-ft. circle
		30-yard lob pitch	Sand wedge	5	1 in 4-ft. circle 4 in 8-ft. circle
Bunker	5 minutes	20-yard short bunker	Sand wedge	5	2 in 4-ft. circle 3 in 8-ft. circle
		40-yard long bunker	Sand wedge	5	1 in 8-ft. circle 4 on green
Putt	7 minutes	3 feet	Putter	8	Make 6
		24 feet	Putter	8	8 in 4-ft. circle
		45 feet	Putter	8	5 in 4-ft. circle 3 in 8-ft. circle
Creative shotmaking	5 minutes	You select	You select	5	You decide

YOUR GAME-TRACKER, THE SCORECARD

Another helpful tool in measuring your progress is your scorecard. If you've never enjoyed keeping score, perhaps it's because par is a totally unrealistic goal for you (at least for now). Set up a better measurement system simply by asking yourself what you think you should shoot on the course.

Double-bogey golf? That's two over par on every hole, so draw a line through the par printed on the card and record your own. Every par 5 becomes a par 7, every par 4 a 6, and every par 3 a 5. After allotting yourself two putts on each hole, you've got the rest of the shots to get to the green. Now you can play smarter golf. Who needs to play that risky shot over the creek and around the bunker when you've got five to get to the green? Play away from trouble and "zigzag" to the hole. Nobody said you had to be a conventional golfer to be a good one. Draw your own road map to the hole and see how well you can score compared to "your" par.

Your Scorecard

Hole No.	1	2	3	4	5	6	7	8	9	Out
Par	4	4	4	3	5	4	4	3	5	36
Your par	6	5	6	6	7	5	6	6	7	54
Your score	6	5	7	5	7	6	5	6	7	54

Hole No.	10	11	12	13	14	15	16	17	18	In	Total
Par	4	4	5	3	4	4	4	3	5	36	72
Your par	6	6	5	7	5	6	6	6	7	54	108
Your score	6	6	6	5	6	6	6	6	7	54	108

You shot even par today. Good for you! You had a great day! Celebrate.

As you progress, set your par lower and lower. Go from double-bogey golf to bogey and shoot 90. Then try for 84, then 80, and so forth. Who knows how good you can become!

You can also keep stats on the course to indicate what you are doing well and what areas of your game need the most work. Stats

are great for list-makers, but keep them simple so you will record
them each time. The beauty in this is getting a comparison from
round to round.

Here's how to use your card's score box for each hole to track
your round: Put your score in the middle. Place a ✔ in the top left
corner if you hit the fairway on your tee shot. Put a • in the top right
corner if you hit the green in the regulation number of shots
(based on "your" par). Record the number of putts in the bottom
right corner. After your round, total up the fairways, greens, and
putts, and record them on a master sheet. It's also a good idea to
indicate what you did best on each hole or what kept you from
making your par. This way you know what you need to work on and
maintain on the practice tee.

Each of these measurement systems will help you build confidence, and you need that to think your way to lower scores. Let's
see how you do as you put them in action.

HOMEWORK

Set three short-term goals and one long-range goal for your game
after this 12-day program is over. Write them down twice. Tape a
copy to your mirror and carry the other one with you. Read over
them every day for the next 90 days. On day 91, reassess your goals.
See how you did and reward yourself if you've done well.

DRILLS FOR THE PRACTICE TEE AND THE COURSE

• Warm up.

• Do the 40-minute practice program based on your handicap
level. Spend 15 minutes extra on the weakest part of your game.

• Play nine holes, keeping your stats and setting a par that is right
for you. Mark your scorecard with your new par before you tee off.
See how low you can shoot playing smart golf.

Sample Scorecard (Front Nine)

Hole No.	1	2	3	4	5	6	7	8	9	Out
Par	4	3	4	4	5	3	5	4	4	36
Your par	6	5	6	6	7	5	7	6	6	54
Your score	6 2	5 3	6 2	4 2	7 4					
	W-irons / M-tee shot	W-putting / M-tee shot	W-fairway	M-chip	W-3 / good hole!	M-putting / W-short irons				

Legend: M = Maintain; W = Work on

Stat Master Sheet

DAY	PLACE	NO. OF HOLES	SCORE	FAIRWAYS	GREENS	PUTTS	COMMENTS

THE 40-MINUTE PRACTICE PROGRAM AND KEEPING SCORE

- Set goals, perform, and evaluate.
- Set short-term and long-term goals.
- Reward yourself when you reach a goal.
- Practice the 40-minute program whenever you go to the range. Always spend 15 extra minutes on your weakest area, following the routine.
- Goals help you measure progress and improve your confidence.
- Create your own par based on your ability.
- Keep stats to indicate strengths and weaknesses from round to round.
- The better you do in practice, the lower the scores you can expect on the course.
- You don't have to be a conventional golfer to be a good one.

SWING KEYS

"Practice your weak areas and maintain your strengths."

"Use your imagination and create shots."

"Practice with a purpose."

"It's quality, not quantity."

"Practice like you play and you'll play like you practice."

DAY 12

Games to Make Improving Fun

Today is the party at the end of the program! School is out, so it's time to play games. Here are a few you can play at the practice tee and others you can play on the course. Some you can play by yourself, while others require a partner. Get your friends to play along.

Games are not only fun, they also help you improve without your even realizing it. You focus so much on the game within the game that you stop thinking about mechanics and just try to score. Some games you'll be better at than others. Everyone's got strengths and weaknesses. Just keep playing an assortment so your whole game develops in the midst of the fun. You can even make up your own games. Just look at the weak areas in your game and design a contest that will help you improve. Contests add pressure similar to what you experience on the course. You'll be that much more prepared to meet any challenge.

GAMES FOR THE PRACTICE TEE: PUTTING

The Clock

Using 12 balls, make a three-, four-, or five-foot circle around a hole simulating a clock. Start at the one o'clock ball and putt until you hole out all your balls. If you miss a putt, you must put the ball back in the clock. For example, if you miss the three o'clock ball, replace the ball, then continue around until you get back to three o'clock and try again. See how few times you can go around the clock and make all your putts. Challenge a friend at a different hole and see who finishes first.

Sevens

You need a partner to play this game. After deciding who goes first, each player putts to a selected hole. You earn one point if you're closest and two if you hole it. The point leader selects the next hole. The first player to earn seven points wins. If you go over seven, you lose all your points and must start again at zero. Subtract a point for every three-putt.

Hole That Putt

Play this like the game show "Name That Tune." Challenge a friend to hole a putt starting at three feet. Her challenge to you must add at least one foot to the distance. Player One: "I can hole that putt from three feet." Player Two: "I can hole that putt from four feet." Negotiate until someone says, "Hole that putt." If the putt is made, the player who makes the claim gets the point. If the putt is missed, the challenger gets the point. Five points wins, but you must win by two.

Lagger Up

Play nine long holes on the putting green, attempting to get every putt within a four-foot circle of the cup. Every time you do, count one. Every time you don't, count two. Set a target score before you play, then see how low a score you can shoot. Challenge a friend. The player who strokes her putt closest to the hole wins one point; second place gets two points. The player with the fewest points at the end wins. If you tie on a hole, you each get one point.

Bogey

This game is played like the basketball game "Horse." Play with a friend or a group. Someone starts by selecting a shot that everyone must hit. The player whose ball ends up farthest from the target gets a letter "B." The player closest to the target calls the next shot. When a player spells "Bogey," she is out. The last player in the game wins.

Blind Lady Luck

Putt nine holes on the putting green with your eyes closed. You may look up at the target before you putt, but close your eyes to make your stroke. This helps connect what you see with what you feel. See how low you can shoot. Challenge a friend.

GAMES FOR THE PRACTICE TEE: SHORT GAME

Hoot and Scoot

Play this game with other players, with each person using a ball clearly marked as her own. Select your first target hole and have one player toss all the balls off the green simultaneously. Each player then hits her ball from where it lies to the target hole and putts out. Low scorer wins a point. Break ties with a chip-off in which the player closest to the hole wins the point. The point winner on each hole selects the new target hole and tosses the balls. Play to five.

Pick a Club

One player starts by selecting a target to hit toward and the club everyone must use. All players use the same club. For instance, "This is a sand-wedge shot." The player closest to the target earns a point and calls the next target and club. The first player to 10 wins. A great game to spark your imagination.

Up and Down

Place nine balls around the green in nine different situations. Find uneven lies, heavy rough, fairway, fluffy lies, and so on. Play each ball by hitting a short-game shot and putting out. Keep score and see how many balls you can get up and down.

High/Low

Challenge a friend to play this game. Use your sand wedge. One player starts by hitting a shot toward a target, then challenges the other player to hit a ball either higher or lower than her shot. If the second player successfully performs the shot, she gets a point. If she misses, the challenger gets the point. Play to 10. You must know what makes a ball go high or low to be good at this game.

GAMES FOR THE PRACTICE TEE: FULL SWING

Par-Tee

Use your imagination and "play" holes on the practice tee. Pick two markers on the range to designate the width of your fairway and hit a tee shot. If your ball lands within the markers, score 1. If outside, score 2. Next, select a green-sized target. If you hit the green, score 1. If you miss, score 2. Play six holes and see how low you can shoot.

Percentages

Hit 10 balls at a target with a particular club and count how many hit your target. Add a zero to your score to give you an idea of what you can expect on a given day on the course. For example, if you hit seven of 10 wedge shots onto a green in practice, you can expect to hit the green with your wedge during play about 70 percent of the time. As you improve, your confidence will grow.

Call Your Target

Play this game with a friend. To start, one player calls a target, then you both hit a shot at it. The player who comes closest wins a point and calls the next target. Play to 20.

Create a Shot

Spend 10 minutes hitting shots with a variety of ball flight patterns, calling each shot before you hit it. Hit hooks, slices, pulls, fades, draws, and even an intentionally topped shot. It's fun and it pays off. You must know what produces the different flight patterns to be good at this game. Once you learn, you can help fix your own swing problems.

The Timing's Right

Work through your odd-numbered clubs, hitting four balls with each club toward a target at 25, 50, 75, and 100 percent swing speeds. This helps you to see where your timing is best and indicates the speed with which you should swing when you play on the course. It also helps to get your swing's natural sequence of motion back on track. Timing and rhythm improve as everything slows down and works together. Don't be surprised if you hit the ball farther and more accurately when you swing at 75 percent speed.

GAMES FOR THE COURSE

Bingo, Bango, Bungo

Play this game within your foursome. The player first on the green receives a point (bingo). The player closest to the pin once everyone is on the green wins another point (bango). The player first to hole out wins the final point (bungo). Three points are given on each hole. The highest point winner at the end of the round wins. This game takes the emphasis off total score and commends you for doing specific things well on the course.

Chapman

This is a modified alternate-shot game for which you'll need a playing partner. After you both hit your own tee shots, you hit your partner's ball for the second shot and she hits yours. Thereafter, you decide on the best ball to play out and alternate shots until you hole out. (The player whose ball is not selected hits the third shot.) A popular game for couples' tournaments.

Fewest Putts

Play a round of golf and keep track of the number of putts you need on each hole. See how few putts you can have and watch what it does to your total score. Obviously, this game highlights your putting, which represents about 40 percent of your score.

Most 3s, 4s, or 5s

Play this game within your foursome and give three rewards at the end of the round: one to the player who scores the most 3s, one for the most 4s, and one for the most 5s. This is just another game within the game that keeps your target focused.

Nassau

Again, play within your foursome and give rewards for the best front nine, back nine, and total 18-hole scores. A long-standing, very popular format.

Point Quota

Earn points based on your score for each hole. Receive one point for a double-bogey, two points for a bogey, four points for a par, and six points for a birdie. Try to earn as many points as possible. Either play this game by yourself and compare your points from round to round or play against others.

Scramble

This is probably the most popular corporate tournament format. You can play this game with two to four players and play for fun or compete against a field of players. Everyone tees off. Your team selects the best shot, and each player hits from that spot. You play in this fashion until the ball is holed out. It's a good idea to play a rule whereby you must use at least six shots from every player per nine to keep everyone in the game.

Skins Game

Play your regular round of golf and give rewards for the lowest score per hole. If two players tie on a hole, everyone ties and the "skin" carries over to the next hole. Even on a day where your total score might not be great, you might win six skins.

Target Score

This is the game that guarantees you'll lower your score! Pick a score you want to shoot—maybe 10 shots lower than normal—and play a round of golf, stopping play when you hit your target score, no matter what hole you're on. The object is to finish your round. Just think, you could play and never shoot over 80 again. The real benefit of this game is that it helps improve your course strategy. With only eight shots left and two holes to play, you'll play really smart golf coming down the stretch.

Three Clubs

To help develop your creativity on the course, play nine holes with any three clubs and see how well you can score. You'll be amazed at the shots you can play around the greens when you are forced to make a shot.

Throw Out

Play a round of golf and throw out the scores of your three worst holes on the front and back nines. A great game to play when you haven't been playing regularly. Everyone is going to have a few tough holes. This game rewards you for the good ones.

THE PEP TALK

Just because golf is a game for a lifetime doesn't mean it should take you a lifetime to learn. The 12-day program you've just completed can be used over and over to get you back on track. The reference sheets will always provide a quick review.

By now you should realize that golf is a game of building blocks. It's tough to pivot if you don't have an athletic posture. You won't cock your wrists if you don't have a compatible grip. Other short-game shots blossom from the basic chip, pitch-and-run, and lob shots. Putting helps your chipping. I could go on and on. When your game is off, check your fundamentals first.

The real secret to becoming a better player is to learn your mechanics, get comfortable with your swing, and trust it. Spend the rest of your time playing creative golf and thinking your way to lower scores. It's just too difficult to dwell on mechanical swing thoughts on the course and still stay in tune with your target. You end up hitting shots instead of playing golf. Work on your fundamentals on the practice tee and at home in front of your mirror, so you can stay focused on playing the game at the course.

Usually you'll see the quickest improvement in the areas of your game that need the most work. At times you'll hit a plateau and have to alter your program slightly to get over the hurdle. That may mean extra time in front of a mirror or around the practice green.

Everyone is entitled to their own goals, whether that means just wanting to have more fun or shooting in the 70s. Just be sure you set goals so you can measure your progress and reap the rewards. Your 10 shots are waiting to fall off. You now have the program to do it. Go for it. On your mark . . . Get set . . . Go!

HOMEWORK

• Recall a course you are familiar with and "play" nine holes of golf in your mind. Imagine yourself hitting a good drive off the first tee and watching it land in the fairway. Base your play on what you would like to do and think you can do. Stay as relaxed as possible and enjoy your good shots. This is called working on your mental game and is the last step you need. See yourself scoring 10 shots lower than usual, then just go out and do it from here on out. It's that simple. You're ready!

COURSE ASSIGNMENT

• Warm up.

• Pick one putting, one short-game, and one full-swing game and play them at the practice area. Remember to bring a friend if you want to play the games that require partners.

• Play nine or 18 holes and play one of the on-course games.

• Reward yourself!

GAMES TO MAKE IMPROVING FUN

Golf is a game that by definition means "a way of diverting oneself; amusement." Keep it that way!

Games to Make Your Practice Time Fun

Putting	Short Game	Full Swing	On the Course
The Clock	Hoot and Scoot	Par-Tee	Bingo, Bango, Bungo
Sevens	Pick a Club	Percentages	Chapman
Hole That Putt	Up and Down	Call Your Target	Fewest Putts
Lagger Up	High/Low	Create a Shot	Most 3s, 4s, 5s
Bogey		The Timing's Right	Nassau
Blind Lady Luck			Point Quota
			Scramble
			Skins Game
			Target Score
			Three Clubs
			Throw Out

SWING KEY

"Have fun."

Sandy LaBauve

Sandy LaBauve, Class A member of the PGA and the LPGA Teaching and Club Professional Division, has been a teaching professional at Stonecreek, The Golf Club, in Phoenix since 1988. Recognized in 1991 as one of the top 50 instructors in the country by *Golf* magazine, Sandy is now featured on the USA Network show *The PGA Today*. She is executive director of the National LPGA Junior Girls Golf Club.

George Kehoe has been editor at *Golf for Women* magazine since its inception in 1988. He lives in Oxford, Mississippi.

Develop Your Golf Skills with
Perigee's How-to Guides for the Weekend Golfer

Break 100 in 21 Days
by Walter Ostroske and John Devaney
For men and women golfers who play mostly on weekends, here's a superfast, easy-to-follow program for shooting in the 80s and 90s, which can be mastered in just 21 days.

Correct the 10 Most Common Golf Problems in 10 Days
by Walter Ostroske and John Devaney
The first book to pinpoint and correct the 10 most common golf problems that hinder a golfer's swing—all in just 10 days!

Master Your Short Game in 16 Days
by Walter Ostroske and John Devaney
Follow a 16-day program to improve your approach to the green and, in the process, lower your handicap!

Power Swing in 15 Days
by Walter Ostroske and John Devaney
Following golf pro Walter Ostroske's instructions, golfers will rid their games of weak shots forever—all in just 15 days!

Two-Putt Greens in 18 Days
by Walter Ostroske and John Devaney
This guide offers an easy-to-use daily program that can be completed in 18 days, erasing forever the three-putt greens from your game.

These books are available at your bookstore or wherever books are sold, or, for your convenience, we'll send them directly to you. Call 1-800-631-8571 (press 1 for inquiries and orders), or fill out the coupon below and send it to:

The Putnam Publishing Group
390 Murray Hill Parkway, Dept. B
East Rutherford, NJ 07073

—— Break 100 in 21 Days	399-51600-X	$8.95
—— Correct the 10 Most Common Golf Problems in 10 Days	399-51656-5	$8.95
—— Master Your Short Game in 16 Days	399-51861-4	$8.95
—— Power Swing in 15 Days	399-51797-9	$8.95
—— Two-Putt Greens in 18 Days	399-51747-2	$8.95

Subtotal $_____

Postage and Handling* $_____

Sales Tax (CA, NJ, NY, PA) $_____

Total Amount Due $_____

Payable in U.S. funds (no cash orders accepted). $15.00 minimum for credit card orders.

*Postage and handling: $2.50 for 1 book, $.75 for each additional book up to a maximum of $6.25.

Enclosed is my   ☐ check   ☐ money order
Please charge my   ☐ Visa   ☐ MasterCard   ☐ American Express

Card # _____ Expiration Date _____

Signature as on charge card _____

Name _____

Address _____

City _____ State _____ Zip _____

Please allow six weeks for delivery. Prices subject to change without notice.

Refer to code #64